She Sheds

She Sheds

A ROOM OF YOUR OWN

ERIKA KOTITE

COOL
SPRINGS
PRESS

MINNEAPOLIS, MINNESOTA

Quarto is the authority on a wide range of topics.

Quarto educates, entertains and enriches the lives of our readers—enthusiasts and lovers of hands-on living.

www.quartoknows.com

First published in 2017 by Cool Springs Press, an imprint of The Quarto Group,
401 Second Avenue North, Suite 310, Minneapolis, MN 55401 USA.
Telephone: (612) 344-8100 Fax: (612) 344-8692

quartoknows.com
Visit our blogs at quartoknows.com

Cool Springs Press titles are also available at discount for retail, wholesale, promotional and bulk purchase. For details contact the Special Sales Manager via email at SpecialSales@Quarto.com or by mail to The Quarto Group, Attn: Special Sales Manager, 401 Second Avenue North, Suite 310, Minneapolis, MN 55401 USA.

10 9 8 7 6 5 4 3

ISBN: 978-1-59186-677-0

Library of Congress Cataloging-in-Publication Data

Names: Kotite, Erika, 1962- author.
Title: She sheds : a room of your own / Erika Kotite.
Description: Minneapolis : Cool Springs Press, 2017.
Identifiers: LCCN 2016033753 | ISBN 9781591866770 (hardback)
Subjects: LCSH: Sheds. | Outdoor living spaces. | Interior decoration. |
Women--Homes and haunts. | BISAC: HOUSE & HOME / Outdoor & Recreational
Areas. | HOUSE & HOME / Design & Construction. | HOUSE & HOME / Decorating.
Classification: LCC NA8470 .K68 2017 | DDC 725/.372--dc23
LC record available at https://lccn.loc.gov/2016033753

Acquiring Editor: Mark Johanson
Creative Director: Laura Drew
Project Manager: Caitlin Fultz
Art Director: Cindy Samargia Laun
Book Design: Shubhani Sarkar, Sarkar Design Studio
Book Layout: Erin Fahringer
Cover photography: Kim Snyder (www.kimberlyjoysnyder.com)
Cover stylist: Dana O'Brien (www.RecycledGreenhouses.com)

Shutterstock: 10 (Mikael Broms), 18 (imnoom), 36 (Monkey Business Images),
76 (Alena Ozerova), 94 (Alena Ozerova), 110 (Enrika Samulionyte), 171 (Reinhard Tiburzy)

Printed in Canada

Acknowledgments

Writing this book opened up to me an entire universe of friendly and generous she shed owners—generous with their time, advice, and singular stories of she shed living. I feel as though I have traveled the world, having adventures and acquiring new ways of thinking about physical space and sustainable living along the way. This book is all about you, blazing trails with your she sheds so that others may get inspired and join the movement. Thank you for opening your doors when I knocked.

There are a few people who really helped me in the early stages of she shed gathering. Jeff Doubet of Santa Barbara Home Designer provided several terrific she sheds and lots of good advice. Dana O'Brien of A Place to Grow/Recycled Greenhouses assured me I didn't want to overlook her unique she sheds (and she was right). I enjoyed meeting Gardensheds.com's Ken Smith and swapping stories with him of the years I lived in beautiful central New Jersey. To my friend Linda Wilson, who has tirelessly introduced me to some of the most beautiful properties and artists to write about since my years at *Romantic Homes* and *Victorian Homes*, thank you for your enthusiasm and encouragement.

Editor Mark Johanson, you took a chance on a new author and gave me a great deal of creative freedom, a courageous stance that did not go unnoticed. I learned a great deal from your calm guidance. Bryan Trandem, you too wanted nothing more than to shape this book into the best it could be; knowing that helped me through more late night and early morning writing flurries than I care to admit.

To my husband, Tim, my daughters, Elizabeth and Caroline, and my son, Dana—you will never pass by another shed in your life without taking a picture of it to show me. Your love and support and quiet tiptoeing past my office because "Mom is writing—be quiet!" are woven in and out of every paragraph. Thank you for helping me complete the book and enjoy every minute of it.

And finally, in memory of my brother Garwood and my sister Gabrielle—recollections of our childhood forts and castles surely contributed to the magic contained within these pages. I will miss you and love you always.

—Erika Kotite

Contents

Introduction

Your Own Little Piece of Heaven

SHE SHED. HEN HUT. LADY LAIR.
Call it what you want, the newest iteration of a woman's private space is looking more and more like a small-but-splendid room built in the backyard. She sheds are mushrooming on properties near and far in a wonderful array of sizes, styles, and uses. From Australia to Alaska, Texas to Ukraine, women are staking claim to a completely personal space to call their own.

The beauty of a she shed is its small footprint, making it easy to fit onto your property and still afford a unique getaway for your creative pursuits—gardening, meditating, reading, painting, or simply hearing yourself think. Most she sheds are built with simplicity at the forefront. They are often not insulated but stocked instead with cozy quilts and pillows. Light is supplied by the sun or maybe by a few battery-operated lights. The idea is to be free of responsibility, using the space to unwind and to do exactly what you want.

Part of the fun of a she shed is using salvage and recycled finds. You'll finally have a perfect use for that wonderful carved door you bought at an estate sale five years ago. Your shed provides the space for that collection of old clocks or tinted seltzer bottles buried in the closet.

As women, we handle a heavy load of responsibility: jobs, marriage, children, household chores, and social obligations. Often we are part of the "sandwich generation," in which we take care of both our young ones and our aging parents. Days will go by in which we must ask ourselves, "Have I had one minute alone, in the quiet, to myself?" She sheds are a refuge of comfort, filled with promise and your treasured possessions. They are there for however you want to use them. A she shed is for you, and you alone.

In this book you'll discover she sheds from around the world, exquisite in their uniqueness, all owned, designed, and enjoyed by women. If you are fantasizing about building your own she shed, consider this a reality guidebook for gathering ideas and seeing how others brought their sheds to life.

If, on the other hand, you just feel like entering into these tiny homes through the pages of this book as enjoyment and fodder for your dreams, that's fine too.

Whatever your desire, you are welcome here.

1 | *What's Your Shed Style?*

If you were to create your own she shed, what would it look like?

Sheds are by definition very practical, no-nonsense little structures. Derived from the Middle English word *shade*, a shed exists primarily for protection—a dry sheltered place to keep things safe.

This practical nature is still very present today even in the most stylish sheds, and for good reason. Keeping the shed's inherent function is intrinsic to its appeal as a she shed. Each woman who possesses a she shed has her own personal reasons for using it. Usefulness is the real beauty in these structures, even if that usefulness includes serious naptime.

That being said, a woman's joy comes not so much from the architectural style of the shed's exterior as from the soul of its interior. Windows and French doors bring in the light of a spring day. Shelving provides a long-awaited place to put family photos or keep jars containing your go-to artist brushes.

No matter how your shopping list of must-haves compares to your budget, there are dozens of ways to modify, make do, salvage, and repurpose. Even women with money to spare enjoy the challenge of creating a haven for practically nothing.

So your shed style will evolve from the functional into its ultimate form. There are a few overarching shed styles that you can consider and some building tricks to achieve them that are within reach and affordable.

Modified Utility Shed

Most kit shed manufacturers provide a no-frills "utility shed" that is meant to serve a variety of functions. This is a shed that begins with a simple wall framing construction, a roof that is high enough to allow for a person to walk upright into the shed, and a single window to let in light. It is basic on purpose: the intention is to make it easy for you to customize it as you see fit.

Think of this shed as a starting point. It provides the floor, walls, and roofing that you require, but it needs your imagination and elbow grease to bring it into full she shed mode. From foundation to rooftop, there are dozens of ways to upgrade and personalize the structure.

For example, instead of laying flat on the ground, your shed can be raised up and given a specialty floor option, such as vinyl or laminate.

The exterior siding might consist of either basic flat plywood panels or shiplap siding. Shiplap siding is often installed vertically (think about a barn), but it can also be turned on its side to create a sleeker, more modern look. You can also add decorative trim and give it a two-color paint scheme.

The kit window is usually made of thin glass or even plastic, so it can be replaced with a true operating window. Sheds usually have very wide or double doors, but you can opt for a beautiful French door instead.

Modern

The modern look is most often equated with minimalism—straight lines, no frills, and a restrained palette with maybe one bright note of color here and there to keep things interesting.

Modern-style sheds are often built of horizontal wood siding or larger rectangular panels—aluminum, acrylic, and other modern materials are common as well. The roofline is flat or minimally sloped. Windows are large, single pane, and simply framed; upper-level clerestory windows and skylights satisfy the style's natural light requirement. Decorative elements might include abstract sculpture or a tapestry of native or geometric design.

Another very appealing element to modern style is the removal of barriers between outdoors and indoors. Besides the large windows, many modern-style sheds have single or double glass doors opening out to a front deck.

Romantic/Vintage

If Pinterest is any indication, the romantic/vintage aesthetic is probably the most popular in a she shed. The look is deeply feminine, borrowing from the still-thriving shabby chic tenets of muslin slipcovers, distressed antique furnishings, cabbage roses, and sparkling chandeliers. This style goes very well with Victorian architecture, especially Gothic; it's also a good choice with a simpler cottage-style shed.

A romantic style accommodates women who collect china, art, fabrics, jewelry, or antique silver pieces. The collections become part of the design. Women with romantic-style she sheds experience a deep satisfaction in finally having a place of their own to decorate that doesn't have to take into account anyone else's opinion or style.

Classic

The classic style varies from country to country. It is essentially the home style that we each imagine in our minds, an etched impression we've had since childhood. Very often, a classic she shed will mimic the lines of a woman's home—similar siding, window shapes, and roofline.

Think about the traditions of architecture in your own area. Does that sense of connection with home and country appeal to you? If you want a shed that serves more as a "second home" in your life, then a classic design approach could work well. Classic she sheds attempt to provide similar amenities of a proper home, on a smaller scale.

Rustic

The rustic she shed holds a particular beauty in its utter lack of finesse. Weathered, quirky, and eclectic, these structures appear to have sprung organically out of the ground where they sit.

Whether you are a nature lover or simply one who hates waste, the rustic design is appealing in that it embraces near 100-percent sustainability. These are sheds built with a hodge-podge of salvaged materials, donated windows, and leftover furniture from the house. What's astonishing is how beautiful the end result can be.

These are by no means the only styles to consider. They offer advantages and ideas that you can incorporate or even layer. You will find—if you haven't already—that visual cues and examples will be the building blocks on which you will plan your own space.

Anatomy of a Shed

No matter what the style and function, a shed is constructed with essential components. You can think of it like a stripped-down version of a small home.

Foundation. This is where it all begins. Your foundation supports the entire shed and keeps it firmly in one place. You'll find more information on foundations in Chapter 7, but there are three types to consider: skid, slab, and raised (or pier).

⁃ A skid foundation rests on a gravel bed and consists of two or more 4×4 beams with the floor frame built on top.

⁃ A slab foundation is a level platform made of concrete that is poured into a wood frame about 6 inches in depth. The slab rests directly on top of the ground and can be used as flooring, or you can build a floor on top of it.

⁃ A raised foundation rests on four piers—concrete cylinders dug partially into the ground for stability. The piers support the floor frame of the structure.

Which one is right for you? First check with local building codes to see if there are any rules for outbuilding foundations. Then you might seek the advice of a knowledgeable builder in the area. Slab and skid foundations are probably the easiest and least expensive to build, but raised foundations provide better protection from ground moisture and are good options on a sloped site.

A floor plan. Most she sheds are single rooms of a square or rectangular shape. They have no interior walls; half walls and other partitions can be added to conceal a storage area.

Walls. Walls consist of framing lumber, usually sheathed with an exterior-grade plywood panel. Most sheds do not have insulation or drywall. Instead, the stick wood framing is left exposed, providing rustic charm and ad hoc shelving on the nailers (horizontal studs).

Doors. Since they are designed to house large items, sheds are often designed with wide or double doors. Kit sheds usually come with simple swing-out doors, hung with heavy-duty metal hinges. Custom sheds often incorporate doors with glass, either single-pane or French style. Another fun option is a Dutch door, which is divided in half horizontally so you can open just the top for light and air.

Windows. Larger kit sheds (8×10 feet or more) will usually have at least one window in their design. The "glass" may be actual glass or acrylic. Most she shed owners will add or modify their windows, and it's not difficult to do. Pay attention to window placement for optimal light, ventilation, and privacy.

A well-built shed is sturdy, watertight, and comfortable. A she shed should be tall enough for comfortable standing, roomy enough for simple furnishings, and equipped with windows for light and ventilation.

2 | *Sheds for Gardeners*

One of the most popular pursuits for the she shed owner is gardening. What a boon it is to have a dedicated space for storing gardening tools, potting new plants, poring over seed catalogs, and even nurturing seedlings. Whether your property is large or small, a gardening shed fashioned just the way you want it creates a natural punctuation mark, even a focal point for the landscape.

Gardening sheds often straddle the line between potting shed and greenhouse. Classic greenhouses are crafted with glass panels—today's versions are often constructed with polycarbonate panels that let in soft, diffused light and also trap air, which helps regulate the temperature inside. You can make your greenhouse comfortable with a worktable and seating, then use it to propagate seedlings through the cold winter months.

Putting the "she" in a gardening shed means adding a little something extra—a comfortable place to sit, a few decorative touches, or maybe collections that celebrate the art of gardening. Oh, and a vase or two for all those fabulous dahlias you'll be growing.

Corncrib Conversion

The common corncrib, once a staple on every farm, has gone the way of ice houses and haystacks. These ingenious little sheds were constructed with open chinks between the slats so that air could circulate to both dry the corn and keep it free from rot.

One such corncrib was saved from teardown on a homeowner's property in Eastern Shore, Maryland. Instead, architect Jon Braithwaite and interior designer Jamie Merida asked landscape designer Geoffrey Stone if it could be worked into his classical garden scheme. The answer was yes—beautifully so.

The corncrib was moved to become an anchor in a European-style parterre garden. The building crew removed rotted wood and installed a standing-seam metal roof to keep it watertight. Windows were cut into the walls, and shelves and lighting were installed. The original corncrib slats, however, were left alone. The interior remains spartan and has little in the way of elaborate décor—it is a working shed that puts the priority on storage, organization, and offering space to keep the garden growing.

The homeowner was pleased that she could reuse a piece of history on her property and loves the calming quality of the vegetable and cutting garden seen from louvered windows.

Photography: Robert Radifera
Styling: Charlotte Safavi

She Shed at a Glance

Designers: Geoffrey Stone/ Jon Braithwaite

Location: Eastern Shore, Maryland

Type: Restored

Size: 8×12 feet

Time to Build: n/a

Cost: n/a

A falling-down corncrib is made shipshape for a homeowner on Maryland's Eastern Shore. The original slatted walls were repaired and repainted, and two windows were cut out to provide light and ventilation inside.

Saving a Piece of History

If you are lucky enough to live in an historic home, chances are good you have an old shed on the property as an added bonus. Most sheds have been treated as throwaway architecture, and little, if any, time and money is spent on their upkeep. Keep in mind that it's almost always more cost-effective to rehabilitate an old structure than to tear it down and start from scratch, especially if it is a shed.

Sheds and outbuildings are important historic markers that are not given the attention they deserve. According to the Craftsman Blog (www.thecraftsmanblog.com), "Outbuildings, such as sheds, garages and accessory cottages are often overlooked in historic neighborhoods since they are relegated to backyards and tend to have simple designs and small scale. However, outbuildings are a significant portion of the historic fabric of many older neighborhoods, adding a visible layer to the history of neighborhood development."

There are programs in some countries (including the United States) that protect old outbuildings by providing tax credits for improvements costing more than a certain amount of money. Contact your local Historic Preservation office to see if there are tax incentive programs in your area.

(Opposite) Serving as a functional potting shed, the structure's interior is a no-nonsense array of tool racks, shelving, and overhead hanging hooks. One splurge: European copper light pendants.

(Top) The plain-spoken corncrib is surrounded by an elegant parterre garden, yet it all seems to work. Classical touches like this plinth and urn form part of the landscape that surrounds the shed.

(Bottom) Many different plants are cultivated on this large property, and the corncrib-turned-she-shed provides space for storing bulbs and seeds.

Do-Over Gardening Shed

Like most people, Judy Weiss had her gardening tools and supplies in numerous places on her Shelocta, Pennsylvania, property—the basement, the garage, the backyard shed. For many years she made do. Then she looked at the old shed and decided it was time to centralize. "I love gardening and wanted everything to be in one location," Weiss says.

Weiss and her husband began by looking around to see what they already had and how they could use these materials to improve the existing shed. Then they figured out what materials they would still need. They came up with a plan and then started immediately on the project.

The shed was structurally sound but "needed a little TLC." Her husband put a new hip roof on it, then moved the walls to create a front porch. It took him about three weekends to build the roof, move the wall, and side the exterior.

The Weisses used siding left over from another project and did all of the labor themselves to save money on the shed restoration. They had to spend about $500 total on plywood, shingles, paint, and a few other items to refurbish the shed.

A she shed was born.

Weiss spent a week applying two coats of paint on the ceiling, walls, and benches. The large workbenches are ideal for a variety of projects. "I like that I can be in the middle of something and just leave everything laying out until I have time to work on it again," Weiss says.

When she's not gardening, Weiss relaxes on the porch or inside on a wicker chair for some quiet reading.

Photography: Judy Weiss

She Shed at a Glance	**Designer/Owner:** Judy Weiss	**Type:** Restored	**Time to Build:** Two months
	Location: Shelocta, Pennsylvania	**Size:** 11×22 feet	**Cost:** $500

Judy Weiss's homey shed is partially shielded with a trellis made by her husband. "I love when the vines start filling in," she says. The small porch gives her a place to display plants and vintage pieces.

(Top) An L-shaped workbench provides workspace for serious potting pursuits. Shelves were built below the bench to store pots and tools. Large windows on all sides let in plenty of light. The couple also found free salvaged wood, which they used to build the benches. Weiss chose a blue paint for her workbench as a contrast to all of the white walls and ceiling.

(Above) An old coal bucket belonging to Judy's grandfather is now a planter.

Builder's Notes

- Don't think dainty when it comes to gardening shed work surfaces. Weiss used two coats of durable wood floor paint on her workbenches to help them withstand the heavy use of a potting shed.

- Try this door restoration trick: use barn door tracks for easy open-and-close operation. Barn door tracks are also ideal when your door swing-out space is cramped. The Weisses attached two salvaged six-panel doors and put them on tracks to replace the old door in the back.

(Above) When they moved the walls, the Weisses were left with a small alcove. Judy used the space for a table made from an old laundry tub. The curtain panels are made from an old shower curtain bought for $2 at a yard sale.

(Left) Everything decorating the shed came from flea markets, auctions, barn sales, or antique shops.

Mary's Birthday Shed

For years, Mary McCachern was mentally drawing up plans for a she shed to end all she sheds. Finally, on a milestone birthday, she had her wish. On the property of their lakeside home on Lake Norman, North Carolina, McCachern's gabled custom shed sprang to life. Generously sized at 10 feet by 16 feet, the shed was modeled after a little shingled cottage with green trim that McCachern spied on a magazine cover.

The shed took a few months to build, with a raised wood foundation and a small front porch. Inside, the ceiling is open, revealing exposed joists and support beams. All is painted with just one coat of white paint over spruce. The plywood floors are painted the same color as the front porch floor. The shingled exterior has two coats of a semi-transparent stain, with gray-blue tones to quickly "weather" the wood.

A nearby salvage shop called Cline's was the place McCachern found many architectural elements for her shed, including $15 turned porch posts, $3 "distressed" metal panels for the porch roof, and $12 doors.

McCachern's work area is both simple and clever. She designed two workbenches about 2 by 4 feet right next to each other on one wall. The benches are constructed with plywood and 2×4s, painted white. Then McCachern contacted a sheet metal shop that fabricates HVAC ductwork and asked them to design two countertops and backsplashes. The grand total was $75. The final touch was adding curtain fronts made of a floral fabric to create a hidden storage area underneath.

After twenty years in the retail arena, McCachern was armed with a finely tuned sense of style. She happily unloosed a flood of creativity that manifests itself in glorious vignettes reflecting the changing seasons. She uses her shed for plantings and garden work, but McCachern's space is more about a deeply imagined creative environment. It's a place where all of her visions can come to life.

Photography: Mary McCachern

She Shed at a Glance

Designer/Owner: Mary McCachern

Location: Lake Norman, North Carolina

Type: Custom

Size: 10×16 feet

Time to Build: Three months

Cost: n/a

From top to bottom, McCachern's classic shed is ornamented with antique tools, gardening pieces, signs, and wooden elements of the past.

(Right) Keeping old and original patinas is a key attraction in the vintage style. A patterned indoor/outdoor rug covers the floor; McCachern's grandmother's old pink chest got a facelift with clear wax and chalk paint.

(Opposite, top left) The glossy red front door outside reveals a vintage aspect on the inside. Chalkboard messages herald the seasons, and decorative knobs hold more treasures.

(Opposite, top right) Floral fabric creates a soft skirt for the practical potting tables topped with metal sheets. Plenty of windows afford good ambient light year round.

(Opposite, bottom left) Whether it's the front door or the back door, McCachern's she shed is all about the visual details.

Elements of Style

- Plan for one big splurge. For McCachern, it was a pair of exquisite leaded glass windows. One hangs vertically, the other horizontally in true eclectic style.

- An inexpensive but effective decorative element is swaths of landscape burlap found in home improvement stores. Use it to create window swags, soften metal sculptures, or as a rustic table covering.

The Year-Round Potting Shed

In 2007, a huge tree fell down in Becky Sanks-Hogg's backyard in West Linn, Oregon, completely crushing an old storage shed in its path. "My husband and I began discussing how we could replace it with a functional potting shed for me, to keep some of the citrus I grow from freezing." Sanks-Hogg recalls. She pored over magazines and DIY books to find the design she liked. Then they set to work gathering materials.

A remodeler friend donated eleven windows, all matching wood-clad, double-hung units with antique wavy glass. These windows guided the shed's final design. For exterior wall surfaces, they used recycled cedar siding, placing the painted side against the building and then staining the exterior when complete.

The interior wall surfaces are wood that was salvaged from a torn-down chicken coop; galvanized corrugated metal was used for the loft. Sanks-Hogg's husband cut an old wood table in half and mounted it to the wall for added shelving. It is first and foremost a working shed, and everything gets moved around regularly. Electricity, plumbing, and heating were added to make the she shed a year-round structure.

Sanks-Hogg enjoyed collecting pieces over the years to use and reuse: an architectural piece that holds a collection of watering cans, an old faucet to use with her large double sink, and an old cabinet that was donated by a friend. Sanks-Hogg's husband passed away a few years after the shed was complete. "I enjoy sitting out here on a beautiful sunny day, reminiscing of our wonderful years together."

Photography: Becky Sanks-Hogg and Anissa Crane

She Shed at a Glance	**Designer/Owner:** Becky Sanks-Hogg **Location:** West Linn, Oregon	**Type:** Custom **Size:** 12×20 feet	**Time to Build:** Two months **Cost:** $3,500

Stained recycled cedar and sage-green trim form the exterior of Sanks-Hogg's she shed. Note the cast-iron stove leg, repurposed as a garden hose hanger. Her shed won a Green Improvement contest in *Better Home & Gardens* magazine.

(*Above*) Sanks-Hogg uses her West Linn, Oregon, shed to arrange flowers and pot plants but also for relaxing and reminiscing.

(*Left*) The gravel floor is softened with a pretty patterned throw rug. Sanks-Hogg chose to wire her shed so she can use it year round.

(*Opposite*) Eleven pristine double-hung windows helped define the shed's design. Sanks-Hogg's husband cut an unused table in half to create an almost-instant plant shelf.

Her Favorite Things

- **Double sink.** A friend donated the capacious sink (above), which Sanks-Hogg thinks is soapstone. She uses it to pot plants.

- **Water and electrical hookup.** Utilities require permitting, but Sanks-Hogg says it's worth the trouble. "I wanted everything to be complete and functional."

- **Chandelier on a pulley.** "I can raise and lower it to light candles."

3 | *The Artist's Studio*

There is a place near Saratoga Springs, New York, called Yaddo. Since 1926, the large home and grounds has been a retreat and creative incubator for artists from all nations. It was the brainchild of owner Katrina Trask, who, after the deaths of all four of her children, had a vision of how Yaddo could continue nurturing those who seek to leave the world a better place. To date, 5,500 artists have "walked Katrina's woods and found the peace and necessary privacy for creative work."

You will find the spirit of Yaddo in these smaller backyard retreats designed for jewelry making, painting, sewing, multimedia artistry, and other deeply artistic pursuits.

Creating art is usually a messy business, and artists often need large empty spaces to create their work. Most of the artists in this chapter tried to stay within a room in the house but found their creative expression needed a place of its own in which to thrive.

An Eclectic Restoration

When she moved into her Sarasota, Florida, home five years ago, Melanie Van Houten eyed the plain metal shed in the backyard and decided that someday it would be hers. "I didn't have a defined space for myself," she says, noting that her husband had his office and her son had his bedroom. "My art studio was usually on the kitchen table."

Without any building experience, Van Houten set about building interior walls and flooring for the shed. She used scrap wood that was left over from various house and art projects and pieced them together however they could fit. The result is a bit like a homemade quilt. "If a carpenter saw it, he would faint," Van Houten laughs. "Nothing made sense—I used 178 screws and many tubes of caulk in that space—but you know what? It worked."

The "use what you have" mantra held throughout much of the shed's construction. Van Houten found old cabinet doors and bulletin boards to fill some of the wall spaces. She also brought in an array of castoff cabinets and cupboards to create a wall of storage for her art supplies.

One big can't-do-without: air conditioning. The Florida heat inside a metal shed would not be beneficial to Van Houten's joy; fortunately the shed was already wired.

Photography: Melanie Van Houten

She Shed at a Glance	**Designer/Owner:** Melanie Van Houten	**Type:** Restored	**Time to Build:** Two weeks
	Location: Sarasota, Florida	**Size:** 10×10 feet	**Cost:** $500

This little metal shed was already on Van Houten's Florida property when she moved in. She redid the interior and made it into her own art studio.

(Above) The landscaping outside Van Houten's shed is as lush and layered as the interior, adding to the feeling of a retreat.

(Opposite, top) Van Houten found these sweet muslin-clad light fixtures at IKEA. She uses three old chalkboards (which are actually part of the wall structure) as inspiration boards.

(Opposite, bottom left) A clever and cozy trick: layer your shed floors with an array of colorful, inexpensive throw rugs.

(Opposite, bottom right) A self-proclaimed cupboard collector, Van Houten happily placed all of her treasures throughout the shed. Note the odd wood shapes that comprise the wall—Van Houten used old art projects and scrap. Nothing went to waste.

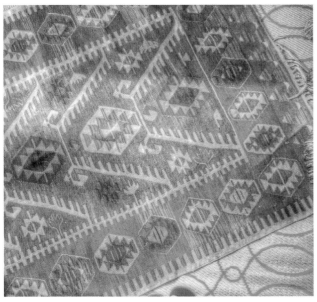

From Greenhouse to Glitterfarm

Jenny Karp is a mixed-media artist in California who also sells organic paint online. The busy wife, mother, and business owner yearned for a place where she could create art and shoot video tutorials. The answer was a shed designed by Dana O'Brien of A Place to Grow/Recycled Greenhouses.

"I worked out the design with Dana, and in four weeks we were ready to go," Karp says. "The rest of the time was spent finding materials and making the money that I needed to build it." Three months later, Karp walked back in to O'Brien's shop with about half the money necessary. O'Brien suggested that Karp look for her own windows and doors instead of purchasing them from her inventory.

A friend of Karp's had some windows stored in her barn. They were fifty years old but had never been used, and she gave them to Karp for the shed. Another friend provided an old French door. With the savings, along with reusing the wood from a pergola in Karp's yard that had to be torn down, the shed's budget was met and the construction began.

Karp wanted an aesthetic that combined the feel of a beach house (she is originally from Hawaii) with the down-to-earth practicality of a ranch. "My mom grew up on her family's ranch, so I wanted my shed to be rustic and mostly made of recycled wood," Karp says.

The shed's design incorporated plenty of windows, including in the doors. With so much natural light, Karp can set up her video camera to shoot from the outside looking inside—the windows open wide for this purpose as well as for ventilation.

Photography: Kim Snyder/kimberlyjoysnyder.com

She Shed at a Glance

Designer/Owner: Dana O'Brien/Jenny Karp

Location: California

Type: Custom (A Place to Grow/Recycled Greenhouses)

Size: 10×12 feet

Time to Build: Nine months

Cost: Approximately $10,000

Jenny Karp's she shed reflects her Hawaiian background and the rustic ranch that her mother was raised on. Wide French doors open onto a spacious room with painted plywood floors.

(Right) The central table is an essential part of Karp's setup and a personal favorite too. Her husband made it from an old desk, adding castors to the legs so Karp can wheel it where she wants.

(Below) The shed's construction includes large windows on both sides and in the back and a double French door in the front. Karp sourced the windows for free from a friend's barn.

Diffused light from the "greenhouse" roof is ideal for Karp's painting and art pursuits.

Karp painted everything with organic paints made from natural chalk and clay, which she sells in her online business, Glitterfarm. Clever storage ideas include this red file drawer with magnetized containers attached to its side.

Builder's Notes

- For shed foundations, a flat surface is ideal (and easiest). Karp laid down unmortared bricks, which are sturdy and also drain water through the openings.

- Keep your shed watertight. Pay careful attention to cracks and openings; caulk everything thoroughly. Doors, windows, and roofs must be built with proper sealing, such as weatherstripping and flashing. If possible, let your nearly finished shed go through a rainstorm or two to see what needs fixing.

- Greenhouses often have semi-transparent roofs made with polycarbonate panels. These corrugated panels allow light in and keep the rain out. This could be a good option for illuminating your own she shed.

Joan's Sun-Filled Studio

Creating one-of-a-kind jewelry in a dark basement was not working for Joan Drews. During cold months, the retired instructional designer would stage her pieces in the basement then bring them upstairs to complete. Beadworking occurred in another room, and the propane tank needed for her blowtorch "was not a compatible roommate" for the room's oil burner and propane water heater. "You might say my she shed was a pre-emptive strike against burning down the house," Drews laughs.

Drews wanted a studio/shed that mimicked the design of their house. She and her husband tore down the deck that was on the site of a former garage and built the shed using the exact same footprint. A few years ago, fungus killed many of the native pines in their area. Drews and her husband decided to mill their own lumber as a way to put the native timber (still beautiful and usable) to good purpose.

They hired contractors to help with the building and install thick insulation. The shed is wired for electricity so Drews can use her jewelry and metalsmithing tools and have plenty of light for her detailed work. One side of the studio gets lots of natural daylight as well, thanks to its southern exposure and a skylight built into that side of the roof. "Discerning slight color variations is vital in jewelry design and beadmaking," Drews says.

People comment that the shed looks like a miniature house, and Drews isn't surprised. "It *is* like a house," she says. "It is built like a house for comfort, creativity, and productivity. I need to be productive, or I feel as though I've wasted time. It's just how I roll. My environment here is comfortable and quiet while I space out and concoct my designs."

Photography: Joan Drews

She Shed at a Glance	**Designer/Owner:** Joan Drews	**Type:** Custom	**Time to Build:** Three months
	Location: Northern Baltimore County, Maryland	**Size:** 12×20 feet	**Cost:** $30,000

All the walls are insulated and finished with drywall. One of Joan's favorite features is the flooring, which is Pergo in wide-plank hand-scraped chestnut—it hides dirt and is also spark-resistant. Her husband painstakingly built the worktable using seven wood varieties and made it a height that was most comfortable for her to work. The red vinyl swiveling soda shop stool was a favorite splurge.

(Above) A retired instructional designer for a hospital, Drews now pursues a dream of jewelry making. Her sun-filled shed is where creations like corsages (at right) take shape.

(Right, top) Two lofts, one in front and one in back of the shed, provide ample space for storage and display.

(Opposite, top) Drews's she shed looks like a mini version of their home in Northern Baltimore County, Maryland. A "small but mighty" front porch creates an inviting entrance.

(Opposite, bottom) The workbench is made for serious work but includes lovely detail. Note the window molding carved with rosettes. Drews added glass knobs to give the spacious drawers a touch of shimmer.

Cindy's Shed by the Sea

A boring and overgrown corner of the backyard was the empty canvas on which fine artist Cindy Goode Milman envisioned her new studio. Together with landscape designer Olaf von Sperl, Milman planned a series of "rooms" that included a she shed as well as spots for reading, a hammock for snoozing, and an outdoor eating area. "I wanted to take advantage of beautiful year-round weather and the smell of the sea wafting from the northeast southerlies blowing through each summer day here in Avalon," Milman says.

Paying homage to the marine setting that she painted and loved, Milman made sure to use repurposed pieces, such as a one-hundred-year-old wharf pole from the old Sydney Harbor, as well as family mementos, including the glass and brass door handle from the well-used entrance of her grandmother's farmhouse.

Because she lives in an apartment building, Milman had to submit plans and wait for approval for her shed. That took about two of the four months necessary to complete it. But the new structure with its green roof ended up a win-win for all. Her neighbors now gaze down on a lush rooftop garden that thrives in weaving-wrapped soil atop polycarbonate panels. Inside the shed, deep green moss creates intricate patterns seen through the panels.

Milman's treasured inlay dining room table, too large for her apartment, is now an integral piece in her shed. It is used often for work (protected with a plastic cover), art workshops, or hosting twilight meals. A reclaimed cupboard offers two large doors for storage as well as ten drawers for separating brushes, pens, labels, and tools.

Photography: Olaf von Sperl/adoremygarden.com

She Shed at a Glance

Designer/Owner: Olaf von Sperl/ Cindy Goode Milman

Location: Avalon, Australia

Type: Custom

Size: 12 square meters (approx. 130 square feet)

Time to Build: Four months

Cost: $15,500 (AUD $21,000)

Milman's artist studio is part of a carefully planned landscape that offers several areas for repose and recreation. A live garden on the roof adds to the magic and also keeps the shed insulated from cold and heat.

Creating a Green Roof

One of the coolest features of Milman's she shed is its living, growing rooftop. Green roofs, as they are called, are roofs that are topped with a shallow layer of soil and planted greenery—often succulents such as sedum, which is a very hardy plant that needs very little care. Succulents lend themselves very well to a shed structure and offer a host of benefits. According to the US General Services Administration, green roofs can reduce storm water runoff rate up to 65 percent; they also stay about 40 percent cooler than standard roofs.

Here are some things to know about installing a green roof on your she shed:

- Green roofs consist of added layers that include single- or multi-ply waterproofing material, a root barrier (such as a pond liner), drainage, engineered soil, and plantings. They add significant weight to the roof and require extra support.

- Low-profile green roofs are not actually gardens but more like a carpet of living plants. They are less needy than a high-profile green roof, which has a variety of plantings and can withstand human activity. (These are found in urban areas and commercial buildings, not usually on sheds.)

- Special soil is required! Your average topsoil is too heavy and may contain pathogens and weeds. A careful blend of clean topsoil, compost, and inorganic material such as perlite will encourage plant growth and facilitate water drainage.

- You can grow a low-profile green roof on a flat or gently sloped roof of up to 30 degrees. Soil depth will be about 6 inches, so you will need a framework that holds the soil in place.

- During the first year, green roofs need regular watering so that the roots establish properly. The best setup is a drip irrigation system, powered by solar panels. You will also need to inspect your roof a couple of times a year for replanting and maintenance.

- Having a green roof professionally designed and installed is a good option for most people; costs range from $9 to $20 per square foot.

She Shed Takeaways

- **Recycled, reused:** door, door handle, windows, storage cupboard.

- **Grand entrance:** bifold doors add a modern sensibility to the shed and ease the passage through the large entrance.

- **Practical:** cement floors, back wall left unfinished to provide shelves for brushes and paintings.

- **Fine details:** Many of the shed's finer details were made or donated by a neighbor.

- **Embedded history:** one corner of the shed is supported by a large wood pole from the old Sydney Harbor wharf (now completely concrete).

(Opposite) This attractive green roof is on a gardening shed in North Carolina. The design calls for a unique grid pattern to hold the soil and plants in place on a sloped roof. *Shelter Green Roof Plans*

(Top) A bevy of "knick-knack kitsch" collectibles on Milman's storage cupboard include seashells and plastic vintage toys.

A Quiet Place to Paint

The first thing you notice about Tamara Armstrong's she shed is the French door painted in a wonderful Dulux color called Magnetic Magic. Personal touches abound, from the door found at a reclamation yard to the single paneled wall that matches the walls in her home.

Her lofty shed, built in a modern style, commands spectacular views of Tamborine Mountain, located in the Gold Coast hinterland of Queensland, Australia. Armstrong, a former high school teacher turned full-time painter, spreads out her paints, brushes, canvases, and anything else she wants while listening to her favorite music. Friends and fellow creatives who were instantly enthralled with the shed asked her to hold creative workshops there; Armstrong assembles groups of four and teaches a variety of topics from drawing and illustration to collage and painting.

The winds kick up fiercely at certain times of the year, making it necessary to use windows with the correct wind grade. "I had saved many photos of small rustic cabins and collected older building materials and windows that I had hoped to use, but I had to be practical and consider a much more modern design," Armstrong says.

Armstrong selected vinyl flooring that mimics wood for its warm look and durability. She spent much time in IKEA, where most of her shelving came from. A rolling drawer cabinet became Armstrong's trusty painter's trolley. "I used to cart my paints around in an old cardboard box; this is so much better!"

Anchoring the interior is a grand old work table that once belonged to Armstrong's grandparents. Armstrong is tall, so her husband boosted the table legs with blocks of wood. He also added caster wheels so she can move it around as needed. "It's my absolute favorite and most treasured piece of furniture," Armstrong says.

Photography: Tamara Armstrong

She Shed at a Glance

Designer/Owner: Tamara Armstrong

Location: Queensland, Australia

Type: Custom

Size: 10×16 feet

Time to Build: Three months (including plan approval)

Cost: $3,500

Tamara Armstrong's she shed has an asymmetrical shape and single-slope roofline; the bold lines are softened with a creamy blue paint that matches her cottage home.

(Above) A single paneled wall displays Armstrong's colorful art pieces, serving as a mini gallery wall for her commissions.

(Right) Armstrong's painter's smock hangs neatly on a hook near the front door.

Builder's Notes

- Consider the climate and weather patterns of your area before building. Heavy rainfall, freezing temperatures, or even strong winds will drive some of your design considerations.

- If privacy is an issue (such as neighbors living just a tad too close), use clerestory windows placed higher up on the wall. They'll let in light and air without letting in uninvited eyes.

(Left) Light floods in from all sides of the shed.

(Below) The compact studio is just roomy enough for a large work table and some storage units. Armstrong splurged on a trio of cage pendant lights to add "just a touch of luxury" to her space.

The Bridal Shed

Stylist Anne Wells creates breathtaking wedding florals for clients throughout the greater London area. She does it all from her little kit shed at the foot of her garden in St. Albans, Hertfordshire. "A shed offered an inexpensive way for me to create my wedding flowers," Wells says.

The shed's plain white exterior belies a beautifully designed workshop inside. Wells made sure the room was comfortable, furnished with a couple of armchairs and a throw rug. Wreaths and flowers bedeck the walls, and the shed is filled with a variety of vases, trunks, and boxes that do double duty as storage or display.

Wells uses her shed as a backdrop to showcase her design talents. "I've surrounded myself with vintage fabrics, ribbons, and finds that I have collected over the years," Wells says. "These help give my clients a clear picture of my creative abilities."

Photography: Anne Wells

She Shed at a Glance

Designer/Owner: Anne Wells

Location: St. Albans, Hertfordshire, England

Type: Kit

Size: 12×20 feet

Time to Build: Three days

Cost: $2,500 (£1,735)

The underside of the roof is swathed in a cotton canopy. (There is a timber roof above.) A storage area to the far end is created with a stud partition that comes out just to the center of the shed.

Elements of Style

Storage isn't usually considered a stylish topic, but when you have a small space, you can't afford to overlook any means of marrying form and function. She shed owners have discovered ingenious ways to keep organized beautifully—read and learn.

- Built-in storage can be comprised of compact cabinetry or open cubbies that are right up against a wall. You can customize the depth so that it comes out just far enough to store the items you want. Take advantage of wall height and build upward to store less-used items overhead.

- Think mobile. Tables and trolleys on caster wheels are great for she sheds because they can be moved easily. Wheel them out of the way when guests arrive or if you have a project that needs to be spread out.

- Need to store lots of drab boxes and bins? Hide them behind an easy-to-make fabric skirt. Attach it to a table or workbench for a practical (and pretty) camouflage.

- Make a simple fold-down table, similar to those found in campers. Attach a sturdy plywood square to the wall with hinges, with a hook to hold it up when not in use. Then add one center leg or two corner legs, also with hinges. The table is there when needed for any purpose and stores flat without taking up any precious space.

- Need a place for long-handled gardening tools such as shovels and rakes? Try turning a castoff pallet on one narrow side and secure it to the wall. Then insert your tools within the open slot on top.

(Opposite, top) A pair of Lloyd Loom chairs are placed near the shed's side entrance, which features a set of divided-light windows and a display shelf overhead. The shelf is simply a ceiling joist faced with a 1×8 plank.

(Opposite, bottom) Wells's she shed is a handy place for running Betty & Bear, her wedding floral business. It provides plenty of room for all of her foliage and tools and is a short commute from home to backyard.

(Above) "The shed is light and airy, relaxing, filled with views of our yard and bird song."

Clare's Sewing Sanctuary

When Clare Mansell and her husband added a second floor to their Chichester, West Sussex, home, they had the brilliant idea of getting a kit shed to use as a temporary sleeping cabin. "I had always fancied some sort of creative space in the garden, but it was hard to justify spending money on," she says. Serendipitously, the sleeping cabin was converted into Mansell's very own she shed when the house was complete.

Mansell opted for a kit shed and searched for a company that would also come out and do the full build. Since she needed it in hurry, she didn't spend too much time worrying over just the right paint color. Two years later, Mansell redid all of the painting and mended gaps where the wood had expanded. The shed is used mostly for sewing and modern quilting. Mansell, a blogger and media professional, also frequently uses the space to get professional-quality photos. The shed's uncluttered white interior offers a perfect photo backdrop; it also serves as an ideal place to watch movies, using a movie projector placed in the loft.

Mansell's walls are covered in mini quilts and other items she has made or that were given to her. "I'm a great believer in the fact that your environment has a hugely positive or negative effect on your life," Mansell says. "Having my shed has definitely made more creative in all areas of my life."

Photography: Clare Mansell

She Shed at a Glance	**Designer/Owner:** Clare Mansell	**Type:** Kit (installed by Creative Living; Oxfordshire design)	**Time to Build:** One week
	Location: Chichester, West Sussex, England	**Size:** 16.5×10 feet (5×3 meters)	**Cost:** $13,000 (£9,500)

Mansell got the idea of using a worktop and kitchen units for the desk from Pinterest. The couch was a triumphant $30 (£20) find on eBay.

(Above) Clare Mansell's shed is heated and insulated because she and her husband originally had it installed as a temporary sleeping cabin while their house was being remodeled.

(Right) A tall cubby on one end of the worktop houses all manner of necessities, including Mansell's collection of sewing and quilting books.

(Above) Mansell uses her she shed for sewing and quilting. "My husband was delighted to get the fabric and noisy sewing machine out of the kitchen!" she laughs.

(Left) With two children, a blossoming business at Maybush Studio, and a huge passion for quilting, Mansell finds many reasons to retreat inside her backyard she shed.

Tool Shed Transforms

Necessity is truly the mother of invention as Anne Freund discovered when she and her husband downsized to a small cottage in Sonoma, California. The jewelry and clothing maker behind The Gilded Gypsies had nowhere to spread out or store her supplies. She needed a place of her own and thought about creating a beautiful little backyard studio.

When they discovered that their homeowners association would not allow a new structure to be built, Freund's husband suggested the tool shed that was already in place. Although uninspiring—the old windowless shed was used to store bags of dirt and trash cans—Freund was game, and the two of them got to work.

Freund's aesthetic leans to the feminine and romantic. She designed the interior around the smallish space that was divided into two "rooms." Her workroom is about 8 by 7 feet, and a storage area on the other side of the doorway is 4 by 7 feet. They cut out a space to fit an antique window they had found and also installed a vintage door that they cut down to fit the shed.

Having tools and supplies in plain sight doesn't bother Freund—in fact, it was intentional. "As visual people, most artists find inspiration from looking at their supplies and stashes of materials," she says. Silver trays and velvet footstools become fanciful displays that always remind Freund what she has on hand to create her Gypsy Jewels and Gypsy Jackets.

Photography: Anne Freund

She Shed at a Glance	*Designer/Owner:* Anne Freund	*Type:* Restored	*Time to Build:* Two weeks
	Location: Sonoma, California	*Size:* 12×14 ft. (divided)	*Cost:* $850

Freund's shed went from trash holder to treasure holder as her jewelry-making studio and sewing room. The old shingled shed got a window, a new door, and unique architectural embellishments both inside and out.

ENTRÉE
DES
ARTISTES

BIENVENUE

(Above) Freund's little studio turns people's heads. "They see the tiny blue door and lace-covered window and long to see what's behind them."

(Right) This jewelry display is made from an old wooden pallet.

(Opposite, top) Freund's husband built this work table and attached it to the wall underneath the window. An antique chandelier and small task lamp add to the natural light. "I think the low ceilings create a cozy dollhouse-like feeling that brings out the playfulness in me and my visitors."

(Opposite, bottom) Old printer trays make handy compartmental storage for jewelry materials.

Builder's Notes

Turning a tool shed into a she shed presents a few challenges; the biggest one is likely roof height. Is it feasible to raise your shed's roof by 12 inches or more? There are several options, but most will likely involve the aid of a structural engineer.

- Extending the walls after raising the roof with hydraulic jacks is one method, but this is definitely something to leave in the hands of experts. A simple wall extension connected to the existing wall won't be strong enough at the point they are connected, so you will need to reframe your walls to the desired height.

- If your old shed has a flat roof, you may be able to convert it to a pitched roof. A pitched roof will add height in the center of the room and it will also drain water more effectively. Use the existing walls and install roof trusses with the desired pitch, then re-roof with the materials of your choice.

- Consider lifting one side of a flat roof and installing clerestory windows. This will add both height and light to your shed. Consult an expert to make sure your old shed can support the modification and to make sure that the modification is done properly.

(Above, left) Silver-plate trays of various sizes are handy catchalls for small items.

(Above, right) Antique wall vases hold Freund's paintbrushes.

Freund prefers using antique cabinets like this spool holder for her supplies instead of new shelving.

Studio for Sketching

There are times when a she shed doesn't start out that way. Susan Mintun, a noted former horticulturist and now a botanical illustrator, knew her tools were losing the battle for garage space with her husband's many automobiles. Nevertheless, she wanted something pretty that reflected the French architecture of her Main Line, Pennsylvania, home.

Mintun contacted Ken Smith of Garden Sheds Inc. and asked if he could modify the company's colonial style shed to meet her needs. The result is both restrained and stylized. "I wanted the 'presence' of a functional structure as part of my garden's design," Mintun recalls.

What she didn't expect was how much she would enjoy being in her new shed. Mintun began using it as a satellite studio to work on her illustrations. She uses an old butcher-block table and sketches away with a view to the flowers in her garden. "If I had known how much I would love this shed, I would have included a sink and maybe insulation so that I could use it year round," Mintun says.

Photography: Susan Mintun

She Shed at a Glance

Designer/Owner: Ken Smith/ Susan Mintun

Location: Main Line, Pennsylvania

Type: Custom
Size: 12×12 feet

Time to Build: Nine months
Cost: $27,000

Ken Smith designed a more steeply pitched roof and included a small oval window and French doors. Two custom-made barn lights in a deep cobalt blue complete the façade.

Her Favorite Things

- French accents: Mintun loves the light that streams in through the French doors, four matching windows, and oval window overhead.

- Copper roof finial, custom made for her shed.

- Fresh wood smell.

(Above) A movable ladder provides easy access to the loft storage area.

(Left) The interior is unfinished, featuring an unpainted cedar floor and one bracketed shelf where Mintun has her collection of birdhouses.

(Opposite) Mintun curated plant collections and taught horticulture in St. Louis before retiring and moving to Pennsylvania.

She Shed Takeaways

If you decide to work with a custom shed designer/installer, here are some key questions to ask in advance before signing the contract.

1. What is included in the package? If you want a company that does everything for you, including all painting and interior finishing, you will need to confirm that. Ask for a complete list, or look on the company's website.

2. Can you provide client referrals? See if the company has a few clients willing to give you their opinion about the product. You can also use review sites such as Yelp to do some scouting on your own.

3. Is my site accessible? This will probably be one of the first things discussed. A completely finished shed will need reasonable access for delivery of materials and installation. An experienced company will have seen many challenging situations. They will likely ask you for photos or a phone video of the access and site area so that they can make a determination.

4. How much will this cost? Truly custom sheds are going to vary widely depending on the materials, size, and the extras you choose. But usually you can get a range of costs per square foot based on the company's experience with past projects.

5. What are your credentials and experience? This information may be on the company's web site, but a conversation with a qualified staff member is also a good idea. Always check out actual references, rather than just relying on website information.

6. Where does assembly take place? Your shed should be constructed and finished in a warehouse or other sheltered environment. Wood components need to stay dry until the paint or stain goes on.

7. Can I build it myself? Often shed companies will either do everything for you or sell you the kit and let you build it yourself. Some will even sell you the design plans.

4 | *Old-Soul Sheds*

What's old is new again. Gently whitewashed by the hands of time, a she shed in the vintage style celebrates the aging process. These sheds may start as new structures but are then transformed into vintage structures with an abundance of details that reflect another time and place.

The use of weathered wood for floors and trim, painted wood doors, divided light windows, natural fabrics such as canvas and cotton, rag rugs, and antique decorative accessories are good ways to capture the vintage look. A bonus to choosing this style for your shed is that so many wonderful things can be found very inexpensively at flea markets, estate sales, and online.

Then there are those old, battered structures in countless backyards, sometimes forgotten and falling apart. While tearing down these structures and building fresh is tempting (and also has several advantages), evaluate the situation carefully before making your decision. If the foundation and overall structure is sound, it might be wise to use what's there. You can merge old and new by tearing out rotted boards and replacing windows. A big part of the shed movement is about respecting the structure's history and avoiding waste.

Allie's Hen Hut

In times past, tending to the chickens may very well have been a rare period of serenity for busy farm wives—a place to think and dream as they fed their flocks and gathered eggs.

The Rieder chicken shed was built next to the chicken coop as a place where Allie Rieder and her friends could come to hang out, help with the chickens, and tend to some of the seedlings grown on the family's Santa Barbara ranch. "I love going out in the mornings to feed the chickens," Rieder says. "The chickens all come running, looking for handouts when they see me opening the door."

The shed's beautiful aged patina is the result of new construction using old materials. Designed in a basic saltbox style, the structure has walls of old barn wood harvested from torn-down barns in the Midwest. Rieder's father, Jim, and a crew of painters used faux painting techniques to create an aged look on the windows, door, and the cupola.

To let in light and air while keeping out errant chickens, the shed has a Dutch door painted a faded white. Simple in aesthetic and in its function, Rieder's shed offers a regenerative space to a busy young woman with happy dreams of the future.

Photography: Jeff Doubet

She Shed at a Glance	**Designer/Owner:** Santa Barbara Home Designer/ Allie Rieder	**Type:** Custom	**Time to Build:** Nine months
		Size: 10×12 feet	**Cost:** Approximately $10,000
	Location: Santa Barbara, California		

Copper detailing on the cupola roof and around the cedar shake roof adds a rich metallic element to the shed.

(Above) To give the "new-old" shed a sense of place, rustic fencing attaches the structure to the chicken coop and garden. The fence gate was made with grape stake boards. Flame grapes grow along the split-rail fence.

(Opposite, top) The interior walls are old redwood planks installed horizontally. Rieder and her friend Olivia share a workbench that was made from leftover barn wood, which was also used to make open shelving.

(Opposite, bottom) A glimpse of the other side of the shed from the workbench reveals that it is also a place for tools and feed storage.

Elements of Style

Ranch life has roots that go back to ancient times as a lifestyle designed to raise and manage domestic animals such as horses, cattle, or sheep. Ranch living is characterized by sweeping tracts of land punctuated by a low-slung house and outbuildings. Capture this open land sensibility with a few of these ideas:

- **Dutch doors.** Dutch doors are one of the most popular features of a she shed. They are both practical and attractive, conveying the timeless appeal of a European farmhouse. Dutch doors can be built new, but you can also convert a single door into a double-hung door.

- **Fencing.** Ranch fencing is designed with three or four horizontal rails supported by posts and often painted white. A more rustic version would be lengths of straight tree limbs, cut into rails and posts.

- **Window boxes.** Wood planter boxes filled with geraniums, ivy, miniature roses, or impatiens instantly transform an otherwise plain shed. Place your plants in a metal or plastic liner and change them out as needed.

Dinah's Rustic Retreat

At 68 and 80, Dinah Lundbeck and her husband don't move as quickly as they used to. Still, the rustic she shed they built on their expansive San Luis Obispo property was completed in less than three months. The structure, Lundbeck says, was influenced by the raw materials on their property and the design of the existing buildings. "We have a village-like quality to our living space, so the separate shed fit in well."

Lundbeck wanted her she shed to double as a guest bedroom and her own retreat to rest and think about her family. She decorated the shed with family photographs that had been packed away for years. The simplified "shabby chic" design worked well for the couple, who are handy but not finish carpenters.

Lundbeck made the stained glass windows; her husband hand-milled the pine siding from pine trees on their property felled by a fungus several years prior. "We felt good about putting those trees to good use," Lundbeck says.

The shed is completely wired with two outlets and lights, including an antique chandelier that glows invitingly in the evenings. Lundbeck enjoys lying on the day bed and communing quietly with family members, both living and gone. "My little she shed gives me the place to honor them and stay connected."

Photography: Sarah Greenman

She Shed at a Glance	**Designer/Owner:** Dinah Lundbeck	**Type:** Custom	**Time to Build:** Two and a half months
	Location: San Luis Obispo, California	**Size:** 10×10 feet	**Cost:** $1,000

A comfortable day bed commands the interior space, and it is surrounded by shelves and a faux mantel filled with framed photographs of Lundbeck's family. Lundbeck made the bed pillows using lace, crocheted doilies, and buttons from her grandmother's collection.

She Shed Takeaways

Want a fully functional guest room or studio that's wired for electricity? Many she sheds are wired so that the owners can enjoy their space through the evening or have the option of electric heat or cooling. You can add electrical service after finishing the shed and using it for a while, but it's a lot easier to build it into the design and construction early on. Just as with a house, wiring a shed must be done by a qualified electrician.

The first step is to consult your local building codes to find out if it is permissible to wire your shed. You may need to apply for a permit and have your final wiring inspected and approved before use. This is actually a positive, as it will ensure your wiring is sound, safe, and properly installed.

Custom-built sheds will have all of the housing for electrical built right into the design, provided you request it. This reduces time and effort, but the overall wiring will still likely have to be approved by permit and inspection.

If you aren't allowed to add electrical service to your shed, or simply don't want the trouble of getting a permit, consider battery-operated lighting. To help keep the shed brighter during the day, build in plenty of windows and perhaps use polycarbonate panels on the roof.

Note how the exposed wall studs, painted in a contrasting color, serve to frame the various-sized photographs. A decorative corner cabinet maximizes space.

Perched on the edge of a canyon, Lundbeck's pine-clad she shed is part guest bedroom, part family gallery. The French doors open fully for an indoor/outdoor experience. Sheers can be pulled down to help screen out insects.

A recycled fireplace mantel makes a wonderful shabby chic-style display shelf.

Lundbeck made the shed's two stained-glass windows herself.

Mary Lou's Colonial Potting Shed

For eleven years, Mary Lou Adams saved photographs of some quaint little sheds she saw in the colonial historic district of Williamsburg, Virginia. The village, with its rich history and simple clapboard structures, stayed in her imagination. She wanted a piece of it transplanted to her Leetonia, Ohio, home.

"My husband didn't want to build a shed for me, but I finally talked him into it," Adams laughs. Using the photos as a guide, Adams's shed was built with narrow cedar siding, square-paned windows, and a steeply pitched roof. But when her husband argued that the cedar should just stay its natural color, Adams balked. "I wanted it a muted gray-green, just like my house," she said.

Adams initially intended her shed to be for potting plants, but it turned out so beautifully that she changed her mind. Instead, the shed is a quiet retreat, complete with a couch, writing table, and elegant decorative touches.

Occasionally Adams hosts summer garden parties, laying tables with white tablecloths, laden with cookies and drinks. But most of the summer afternoons are spent gazing out the French doors on her couch, enjoying the soft sound of the wind through the trees. "It was there when I wanted to get away from everyone and everything," Adams says.

Photography: Brian Snyder

She Shed at a Glance

Designer/Owner: Mary Lou Adams

Location: Leetonia, Ohio

Type: Custom

Size: 12×20 feet

Time to Build: Three weeks

Cost: n/a

An avid gardener, Adams surrounds herself with whimsical garden décor that adds cheer to the somber green walls of her shed. Multiple pathways, border gardens, and landscape vignettes create a beautiful setting.

Should You Build It Yourself?

She shed owners take great pride in the building process. Many a blog offers readers the fascinating story of a she shed coming to life, step by step. It may look really fun—and it is—but the process of laying a foundation, hammering wall studs, and grappling heavy roof panels is also just plain hard work! As with anything there are pros and cons to the decision of whether to go DIY or bring in a professional.

Advantages of DIY Building:

- **Cost.** Usually you will save a lot of money building a shed yourself. Labor is the biggest part of nearly any building project.

- **Experience.** If you are interested in learning about the art of building, then starting with a shed is a great idea. It's smaller and easier than a house. Building your own shed will let you achieve a greater understanding of construction and hone your skills with various tools.

- **Pride.** Some she sheds are built by a husband and wife team, a group of friends, or an entire family with children. The process is long and the work is hard. Much will happen along the way (both good and bad) that will be looked back on with humor and fondness for many years to come. She shed building is an exciting and fulfilling project that takes a village.

Advantages of Professional Building:

- **Ease.** Leaving the design and construction of a shed in the hands of a professional builder is a huge relief to those who are not suited to this kind of work or who do not have the time. Sometimes there is a deadline involved, like the arrival of a new baby that leads to the sewing room needing to be converted to a nursery.

- **Customization.** She sheds are quickly growing in popularity, and as a result more and more companies are refining their shed designs to include generous proportions and better aesthetics. You will have no trouble finding a builder who can add any custom details that you want.

- **Resources.** Shed builders understand exactly what is needed for the most worrisome issues, such as moisture, rot, structural integrity, and safety. They are paid to solve the problems (or prevent them) that otherwise would fall to you.

Take some time to read blogs, leave some comments, and explore the vast world of she shed building in this book and online—the best decision will come to you.

(Opposite, top left) Adams found some long boards and, without any building experience, simply nailed them to the studs horizontally and painted them in a cream color. Her husband taught her how to tape off the wood floor, which she then painted in a dark gray-and-cream diamond pattern.

(Opposite, top right) The main window juts out a bit from the wall, letting in more light and creating a small shelf inside the shed.

(Opposite, bottom) Nestled back on the fringe of her large wooded lot, Adams's colonial-style she shed seems a natural extension of its environment.

Salvaged
She Shed

Many people have old, rundown sheds in their backyard. Jenny Johnston's shed is old but in an entirely different way. The shed was made from scratch with materials that were nearly all salvaged or recycled from other old buildings. The result is an outbuilding that seems right at home, blending harmoniously with its natural surroundings in this East Texas home.

A self-described collector of "junk and treasures" for many years, Johnston finally had the chance to display all of it. She met Mark Gaynor of Living Vintage, whose company creates homes, studios, and sheds out of the salvage they get from old building demolition sites. He and his business partner/wife, Kim, designed the shed using both their own materials and Johnston's. They built the shed on a unique foundation made with upended pavers that create a border around brick. The structure's bottom plate rests on the brick pavers; buried posts that hold up the porch overhangs on three sides of the shed help keep the shed securely in place.

Johnston was ready with piles of images, inspirations, and designs she had been collecting for nearly ten years. Pinterest was a huge source of ideas, and Johnston also joined the She Shed Sisters Facebook group. Living Vintage designed the shed to integrate things, such as Johnston's large collection of old windows and doors.

The end result reflects Johnston's connection with her garden, with times past and present. "I can feel the history and the stories from these wonderful pieces around me," Johnston says. She often welcomes her adult children and her grandchildren into the shed for meals and family gatherings.

Photograpy: Mark Gaynor

She Shed at a Glance	**Designer/Owner:** Living Vintage/Jenny Johnston **Location:** East Texas	**Type:** Custom **Size:** 10×12 feet	**Time to Build:** Six weeks **Cost:** $6,000

Johnston can often be found on her front porch, eating or sipping a beverage, and gazing out on her lush, mature garden. The shed sits on a foundation of one-hundred-year-old bricks.

Builder's Notes

- When working with old lumber, slow and steady saves the boards. Heavy crowbars and hammers are too destructive when harvesting used wood, which is often dry and brittle. Use a small crowbar or a cat's paw to gently remove nails.

- Salvaged brick makes a sturdy floor/foundation, and its warm red color and interesting texture also make it deeply attractive. Here's how to do it:

  1. Use a layer of fine sand about 3 to 4 inches thick (depending on geographic location and soil makeup) as a base.

  2. Start by laying out the floor with a string line at the perimeters.

  3. Set a couple of good straight string lines across different points of the floor as reference lines to keep your bricks straight.

  4. Use bricks that are all the same size for a better-looking floor.

  5. Use 12×12 pavers as borders, positioning them upright and driving them deeply into the ground to anchor the bricks.

  6. Work three or four courses (each course is a single continuous horizontal line) at a time instead of just one. Keep an eye on your string lines.

  7. Gently pound ("set") each brick into the sand so that each one is the same height.

  8. When finished, pour paver-locking sand over the floor and sweep it into the cracks. Do this several times until the cracks are filled. This acts as your grout to keep your bricks firmly in place.

(Opposite) No paint was used on the inside of Johnston's shed. She filled it with children's and grown-up furniture that has history. Burnished old bricks serve as flooring.

(Above) Jenny Johnston's welcoming rustic she shed is made completely—except for four boards—from reclaimed lumber. She liked the remnants of chipped paint on the boards and didn't add any new paint. The twin arched front windows are actually door fronts to a dining room corner cabinet from an older house nearby.

(Left) An old picket gate becomes an outdoor art piece to grace the side porch. All of the beams, posts, and siding are about one hundred years old.

5 | *Stylish Sheds*

Rich with personality, some she sheds defy all standard labels. The stylish shed proves that adding "a woman's touch" to a structure intended for practical use can be transformative in a highly personal way.

While virtually all she sheds reflect the personalities and pursuits of their owners, these stylish sheds are especially potent reminders of how much of ourselves we pour into our private places. A woman's childhood playhouse from times past can lead to an era of stylish expression within and on the walls of a modern utility shed.

How you land on the style that best suits you will depend on your architectural preferences, tempered with a sensitivity to how the shed looks in context with its surroundings. You may have the means to design and build whatever kind of shed suits your fancy, or you may be on a tight budget and must rely on small touches that really count. Either way, the place is yours, all yours, to style just as you wish.

Spanish-Style She Shed

When you think of sheds, you don't usually think of stucco as the most likely building material. Yet here on this Santa Barbara property, a shed built in the Spanish style with plaster and red tile roofing feels right at home. The custom shed was built to mirror the main house on the property and is a miniature tribute to one of California's most popular architectural styles.

"I've always been inspired by Spanish cottages, so I wanted a mini one of my own," says owner Samantha Journey. The owner of an eco-friendly dry-cleaning business uses her shed to dream and plan for things that aren't related to her business. "I have a desk at my shop; the shed is where I go to get away from rules and boundaries."

The shed's luminous sand color is integral to the plaster; no paint was used. The builder worked with someone who had just torn down a very large home; this provided access to substantial architectural salvage, including the windows and the door, which is one of Journey's favorite elements.

Inside, the shed is simply furnished with a countertop workspace, shelf unit, and a day bed. Journey intentionally kept it somewhat spare, allowing the deep gleam of the dark-stained hardwood flooring and plaster walls to foster serenity.

Photography: Jeff Doubet

She Shed at a Glance	**Designer/Owner:** Santa Barbara Home Designer/ Samantha Journey **Location:** Santa Barbara, California	**Type:** Custom **Size:** 10×12 feet	**Time to Build:** Four months **Cost:** Approximately $25,000

Journey's Spanish-style she shed was made with high-quality materials to match the main house. The builder cut costs by using architectural salvage materials, such as the door and windows and even the hardware.

(Above) A wall mural of a large oak tree is the only wall adornment in Journey's shed. "All I have to do is walk in the door and I feel electric," she says. "You don't need to have a large space to make things happen."

(Above, right) The workspace includes a few drawers and shelving, with views overlooking the main house and patio. Salvaged windows are framed by sills sculpted with plaster.

(Opposite) "I love closing my eyes, having the door and window open, and hearing the fountain outside," Journey says. The cupola is plaster with wrought iron detail.

Builder's Notes

Love that Old World plaster look? It's doable for the DIYer but takes extra time, money, and probably some expert help.

- Plaster and red tile roofing are heavy building materials. You will need reinforced framing to support the extra weight.

- Frame the windows and doors keeping in mind the bullnose (rounded) shape of the plaster that is part of the Spanish style. The good news: trim can help camouflage cracks, gaps, and imperfections.

- Consider architectural foam for coved ceilings, curved molding, and other challenging stucco surfaces. These are installed during step two of the three-step process.

A Playhouse All Grown Up

From a very young age, Shirlie Kemp seemed destined to have a she shed. Her creative and imaginative personality was shaped by a father who desperately wanted to grant his daughter's wish to have a Wendy House (a British term for a play house). "He was a builder, so he couldn't buy a kit," Kemp recalls. "Instead, he built me a beautiful tiny house with leaded windows that took up half the back yard."

Kemp's entire childhood and teen years were spent playing either in her playhouse or her best friend's. The fun and memories of those days came flooding back to her in 2010, when she felt that something was missing from her life. "I told my husband that I needed a place where I could go and do anything I wanted and not have to worry about anyone else liking it," Kemp recalls.

Wind Whistle sits on a gentle rise on the Kemps' Hertfordshire property. Kemp hired a builder who built the shed, porch, and stairs. Kemp painted everything white, inside and out, because she wanted to use her shed as a photography studio, and white creates a versatile backdrop. Her husband, a well-known soap opera actor, has had several of his portraits shot there. "No one would believe they were taken in my little studio shed!" Kemp says.

Decorated and furnished in serene "shabby chic" style, Kemp's she shed is the venue of choice for garden parties, iced lemonade on the porch, as well as a busy photography studio. If you visit Kemp's she shed one season, it will be utterly different at the next. Switching out and changing around is what makes Kemp happy and keeps her she shed serving as a stage set for life. Work, play, and "her time" converge harmoniously at Wind Whistle.

Photography: Shirlie Kemp

She Shed at a Glance

Designer/Owner: Shirlie Kemp

Location: Hertfordshire, England

Type: Custom

Size: 10×12 feet

Time to Build: Three weeks

Cost: $5,000 (£3,000)

Wind Whistle is Kemp's brainchild, a continuation of her love affair with she sheds she has had since the age of seven. The simple clapboard structure sits on a raised foundation with stairs and a front porch.

(Above) The shed is well built and withstands rain, so Kemp can furnish with grand pieces like this antique fireplace surround and mantel.

(Above, right) Spring and summer in England are for soaking up the warmth outside. The shed porch is just big enough for a small tea table. Kemp also brings her laptop outside when she can.

(Right) Kemp loves collecting vintage china, furniture, and clothing. "Having a little place to play with them was such an outlet for me," she says. "No matter how old we get, we should still be playing!"

Her Favorite Things

Kemp is an accomplished photographer and stylist. The former vocalist with Wham has a pop music background that blends with her deeply feminine aesthetic in a captivating way. The things she loves best become important parts of the she shed in her life:

- **Costumes and textiles.** Fabrics are everywhere—draped across the day bed, embellishing an old guitar, gracing tables. Kemp's collection includes lace, silk, calico, gingham, and other vintage styles.

- **Flowers.** The advantage of having an English garden allows Kemp to bring in armloads of fresh flowers to her shed. Classic flowers, including roses, ivy, and peonies, are loosely arranged in antique pitchers and vases.

- **Architectural elements.** Clever trompe l'oeil effects in Kemp's shed include an antique fireplace frame on the wall— used not for fires, but as a unique focal point. Kemp revels in the art of using old pieces unexpectedly.

- **China and glassware.** Bits and pieces of old china, teacups, epergnes, candlesticks, and figurines are artfully arranged and rearranged, reflecting Kemp's fond memories of a girlhood spent in her playhouse.

La Casita

When Paige Morse left her full-time job to start her own business, she took stock of her life. "I needed a quiet space to work, but I also needed an additional revenue stream while I was growing the business," Morse says. The answer was staring at her in the backyard—a generous-sized, if somewhat decrepit, shed.

Morse decided to use the shed as a styling and photography studio and then hatched the idea of making it into a sleeping cottage. Her own home went up on Airbnb, and now Morse simply moves into "La Casita" when she has rental guests. She found a contractor who understood how to interpret her visions into a working plan. "I had a vision and he executed it," Morse says. The sheds needed to be torn down to the studs and rebuilt, but the contractor salvaged and reused as much of the building materials as possible.

The structure was plumbed and wired so that Morse could have a fully functional kitchen and bath. The diminutive kitchen is wide open on the back wall, with compact appliances, a few floor cabinets, and open shelves.

Morse spent all of her budget on construction and labor of La Casita. She pinned images of clean, simple Scandinavian cottages on Pinterest for inspiration. Everything on the inside is her own, or given to her, or repurposed.

"This little shed has been my refuge, my safe place in the world," Morse says. "I love that it allows me to rent out my other house so that I can make extra money and have the flexibility to travel and work all over the world."

La Casita is filled with light thanks to floor-to-ceiling windows, as well as the shed's original ceiling air vents, which were replaced with glass. "The light in it is so beautiful throughout the day," Morse says.

Photography: Cody Ulrich

She Shed at a Glance	**Designer/Owner:** Paige Morse	**Type:** Restored	**Time to Build:** Five months
	Location: Dallas, Texas	**Size:** 10×25 feet	**Cost:** $17,000

A rich charcoal paint on the exterior gives the shed some gravitas. The shed was born out of two small, extremely dilapidated sheds on Morse's property.

All of the furnishings are things Morse owned, found, salvaged, or had given to her. The walls are painted bright white.

A stunning chandelier that Morse made from shells hangs over the main living area of her shed. The sofa serves as her bed when she stays here. Handsome wood flooring is mostly original, painted black. Above the beams, a former air vent now serves as a small window.

The dainty sink was found buried beneath another old shed on the property. Morse cleaned it up, added a ticking skirt, and put it in her small bathroom. Flooring is vintage hexagon tile.

Groupings like this are both artful and practical—antique vessels hold extra silverware on one of the kitchen shelves.

Elements of Style

Morse is attracted to a Scandinavian aesthetic that places value on minimalism and pure lines.

- **Contrast.** The shed is swathed in white, with deep black points of contrast: ebony wood floors, throw rugs, kitchen appliances, and entry door.

- **Filtered light.** Lots of light comes through the many windows, softened a bit with translucent muslin panels.

- **Natural elements.** Lacy coral, framed leaves, and a sturdy branch hang from the rafters used for extra closet space.

Morse managed to fit a full kitchen into just one corner of the shed, installing a counter-level refrigerator to maintain a compact feel. Open shelves provide extra storage.

6 | *Backyard Getaways*

This chapter acknowledges the appeal of a place used for just doing your own thing. Whether that thing is resting, thinking, meditating, or hiding, your joy in using a she shed can have a moving, changing definition.

She sheds are places where a woman can let her hair down. Like the childhood treehouse with the sign "No Boys Allowed," here is where a woman finds quiet and privacy. You may decide to open your she shed to the people you love or always keep the door carefully closed— either way it's still quite possibly the only room in the world that is yours and yours alone. Remember that when it comes to she sheds, there *are* no rules.

The sheds in this chapter are used in unusual ways or have an owner who doesn't really designate a distinct "role" for the she shed to play. It's just there at her command, away from the meddling of any other person. It's a meditation room one day, a reading nook the next. Sometimes the shed must be built before its use becomes apparent.

The Tacking Shed

For a woman who loves horses, the needs of her "boys" come first. Kim Manning rides and shows three horses from her home in New Hampshire. Three horses make a pretty large footprint. "We found that we were running out of space," Manning says. "At the same time, we cleared out a large planting in the backyard, and we needed something there as an accent."

An elegant she shed-turned-tacking shed was just what the equestrian ordered. Once she fell upon the idea of a tacking shed, Manning turned to her many architecture and fashion email and Twitter feeds to find ideas. She also drew a lot of inspiration from her travels, where she sought out vintage homes, carriage houses, and interesting sheds with lots of character.

Manning ordered a Williamsburg design from Garden Sheds Inc. in Hamilton, New Jersey. While waiting for the shed to be delivered and installed, Manning had the planting removed and the site leveled, and she planned out the landscaping that would surround the shed once it was in place.

Inside the shed, Manning carefully stores all manner of tacking, which fills several tall metal shelving units. The shed also serves as an award gallery, showcasing the many ribbons and medals Manning's horses have won over the years. She enjoys going inside and looking around as she selects what she needs for the next ride. "I love horses; I love beautiful things, so this shed helps me live out my dreams."

Photography: Kim Manning

She Shed at a Glance

Designer/Owner: Garden Sheds Inc./Kim Manning

Location: New Hampshire

Type: Custom

Size: 10×14 feet

Time to Build: Three months

Cost: $35,000

Manning's she shed elegantly marries form and function. Its design serves as a focal point in backyard. Behind its well-constructed façade, complete with glass-front entry doors, is a full-fledged tack room.

(*Opposite*) Tall shelving units make use of the shed's high ceilings. It also has a loft space for extra storage that is reachable with a small ladder. Manning stores her tack and the supplies that she needs for horse shows as well as day-to-day activity with her horses.

(*Left, top*) Kim Manning with Vigo, one of her three horses. Colorful ribbons and awards from shows and riding competitions decorate Manning's she shed in fine form.

(*Left, bottom*) A picturesque oval window adds visual interest to the shed's facade and shows off one of Manning's many show trophies.

(*Below*) Two entries make access very convenient and allows cross-ventilation on warm days.

Tymmera's Room of Glass

During a trip to Bali, Tymmera Whitnah was captivated by the way many of the houses were elevated on poles. She had a vision of creating her own "spirit house" back home in rural Oregon using the same techniques. It would take many months of patience, lots of helping hands, and a little bit of right-brained ingenuity, but after two years, Whitnah's shed of windows became a reality.

What's unique about Whitnah's shed is that its walls are created quite literally of glass instead of plywood and drywall between the frame studs. While Bali homes are often open to the elements, that was not a practical decision in Oregon with its cold winters. Whitnah pondered her options. "I decided to protect my space with windows."

Easier said than done. Whitnah spent many months scouting construction sites and asking about old windows being pulled out of remodels. Only her drummer friend, who also happened to have carpentry skills, was game to help. "He was the only one insane enough to help me with this crazy idea," she says.

After months spent gathering windows of various sizes, Whitnah laid them all out on the ground and began to assemble the pattern for each wall. Whitnah wanted as many of them as possible to open and let in cross breezes—out of thirty windows used, twenty-two can be opened via hinges and latches.

All the materials used on the shed are recycled. The shed is built on four poles that were hand hewn from lumber found in the nearby mountains. It is furnished simply with a Turkish rug, a wooden box used as a low table, and colored cotton prayer flags fluttering at one of the windows as a valance.

Whitnah uses the spirit house most often for meditation, but during the small parties she often hosts in her backyard, it is a lure for guests to climb up and view the festivities from above.

Photography: Sarah Greenman

She Shed at a Glance	**Designer/Owner:** Tymmera Whitnah	**Type:** Custom	**Time to Build:** Two years
	Location: rural Oregon	**Size:** 10×10 feet	**Cost:** Approximately $600

The first phase of construction for the shed was simple framing of the floor and roof. The roof is clad with corrugated tin found in Whitnah's barn, and a sturdy stepladder made of recycled wood leads to the doorway. Flooring and stairs are from her grandfather's old barn that fell down.

(*Above*) After laying out the pattern she wanted for her walls of windows, Whitnah and her friend then decided whether to cut the windows smaller or add additional 2×4s in between to keep measurements even. "It was very difficult, but I'm glad I did it," she says.

(*Opposite, top*) Whitnah wanted to capture the essence of Balinese living and transplant it to Oregon. Her house of glass makes the walls disappear, leaving only beautiful views and gentle cross breezes.

(*Opposite, bottom*) Simple decorative elements like this valance made of Tibetan prayer flags personalize the shed without detracting from its spiritual purpose.

My Own Little Cabin

When she spends time in her shed, Lori Doubet can hear the wind in the trees. It's the place where she looks forward to taking a break after long hours spent in her two large vegetable gardens. "I'll read, hang out, or mainly just rest," Doubet says.

The shed was built by her husband, Jeff, using a purchased tool shed as a base. An accomplished homebuilder and woodworker, Jeff added custom touches, such as the board-and-batten siding. The couple had several windows left over from an addition they had built, so the shed was designed around them. A painted door salvaged for free from a local homebuilding nonprofit was exactly right.

Once she made the structure her own, Doubet spent a lot of time painting her shed. She wanted a creamy, all-white background both inside and out. Nearly all of the furnishings inside were purchased with gift cards or at thrift stores. Doubet's one splurge was the small-scale sofa that she purchased new.

Doubet lives in Santa Barbara, California, a place that is always sensitive to drought conditions. Around the shed they planted grapevines, which stay green most of the year and need very little water. In addition to vegetable gardening, Doubet also manages most of the landscaping on the property.

Their home is California chic, but the she shed is all about country cozy. Doubet says that the final result is reminiscent of a quiet cabin that the couple visits in Minnesota, where Jeff's mother lives. "It allows me to be girly and country, something I probably wouldn't do in our house," Doubet says.

Weekends are when Doubet can be found in her shed, shoes kicked off and a stack of books by her side. "It's only a small distance from the house but I still feel like I'm far away," she says.

Photography: Jeff Doubet

She Shed at a Glance

Designer/Owner: Santa Barbara Home Designer/ Lori Doubet

Location: Santa Barbara, California

Type: Kit
Size: 10×12 feet

Time to Build: Three months
Cost: $10,500

Doubet's she shed was built using an off-the-shelf tool shed kit. Custom touches include wood siding, extra windows, a painted wood door, and a cupola/weathervane.

The shed snugly fits a sofa, a couple of small tables, and a chair. Doubet found the handmade quilt at a garage sale.

(Left) Doubet painted (and painted) after work and on weekends and helped Jeff install the wood laminate floors. Altogether, the shed took about three months to finish.

(Above) The shed allows Doubet to indulge her "feminine country" aesthetic with cute accessories like these.

Builder's Notes

- Painting wood siding is time-consuming and often takes several coats. Lori Doubet used primer and liked the way the wood emerged through the paint, thus saving a lot of time and labor.

- The foundation for the Doubet shed is simply stamped gravel, meticulously leveled, with the shed's floor frame placed right on top. The perimeter is landscaped with a pretty border of boxwood hedges and flowers to convey permanence.

- Add architectural elements for interest. Doubet's husband ordered a cupola and weathervane online, and they were easy to install. Other ideas include upgraded window trim, corner trim, address plaques and copper rain gutters and downspouts.

- Gather windows and a door before designing your shed (or modifying a kit shed) so that you can get the dimensions right. And remember: measure twice, cut once!

7 | *Build a She Shed from a Kit*

After visiting all of these unique and wonderful she sheds, it's no more than a small leap to appreciating the joy that one could bring to your life. This chapter outlines an actual real-time build of a kit shed and offers an inside look at what it takes for an ordinary person to purchase, build, and furnish one. It begins with a section on the general considerations you need to take into account when planning a kit shed, then moves to a how-to description of how a typical kit shed is constructed.

Finally, you'll read a case study of how one she shed—built in California for Karin Nystrom (my sister-in-law)—went together. No she shed construction goes exactly as planned, and ours was no exception.

Preparing to Build a Kit Shed

Reading about she sheds and actually building one are two entirely different things. There are a number of factors that will directly affect the ease or difficulty of building your shed. These factors will also affect timing and cost.

Local Building Codes

In most of California, where our kit was built, a shed structure can be built without need of a permit if its foundation footprint is 120 square feet or less. This doesn't include plumbing or electrical wiring, however, which will always require permits and inspections. This requirement varies widely from state to state, and even from community to community within a single state. Always check with your local community officials to determine if your shed requires a permit and inspections.

Some of the she shed owners in this book worked with their local permitting laws and sometimes had to modify their plans to accommodate requirements. Having to apply for a permit is not something to avoid or dread. Very often your permit will be approved quickly and affordably. Even if it isn't, temporary rejection is a learning experience—you'll learn exactly why your request was turned down and what to do to correct the issue. Sometimes you might be required to alter your design (making it smaller, for example), or you may be required to move your shed to a different site on the property to comply with setback regulations.

The process may also point out some important steps you need to take, such as avoiding digging around buried pipes. If you are adding electrical service to your shed, the permit will likely require an inspection before the walls are finished to ensure that the wiring is done properly and poses no fire hazard.

Ground Slope

If you have a perfectly level, well-drained plot in mind for your she shed, congratulations and move ahead two spaces. A level building site saves a lot of time. A sloped site will need to be graded to make it level if you want a slab foundation, which will affect everything about your shed construction—time, labor, and money.

Site Selection

Carefully consider exactly where on the property to construct your shed. In the example that follows, the owner had a large, beautiful backyard including a pool with a large concrete deck and pool house. Around the perimeter of the yard is gently sloping softscape with beds of shrubs and flowers. We found a patch of ground near a fun purple gazebo. It took a little time to angle the site just right so that it faced the house and also acted as a privacy element from the neighbors across the way.

The correct location is of key importance when building a shed. Pay close attention to view angles, accessibility, and proximity to other landscape features.

Selecting the site involves these important considerations:

• **Soil condition.** Find a place where the ground is stable and does not collect water.

• **Setback requirements.** There are usually rules that tell you how close you can build to the edge of your property line. This could be anywhere from 6 feet to only a couple of feet or more. You should also be considerate of your neighbors and talk to them about your plans. This is especially important if you think the shed will be in their sightline or even hamper their views.

• **Sunlight.** Catching the light at just the right times will enhance life in your she shed. Usually the ideal direction in which to place your wall with the most windows is southward. A southern exposure provides consistent light throughout the day without direct glare.

What Type of Foundation?

You basically have three choices for the foundation for your shed: *skid*, *slab*, or *raised* (also called *pier and beam*). There are advantages and disadvantages to each.

In the example that follows, a raised foundation was chosen because the site was on a slight hill that provided drainage into a nearby stream. A raised foundation is good for areas where soil can get saturated or may shift. We also liked the look of having a step or two coming down from the front door.

A pier-and-beam foundation rests on piers (cylindrical posts made of concrete encased in biodegradable cardboard) placed in corner holes dug about 2 feet deep. (The depth of your piers will be stipulated by your local building code.) Stone or concrete should anchor it on the bottom. Beams are placed across the floor space from pier to pier, supporting the structure.

A slab foundation has its own advantages. Slabs, usually made of concrete, are laid down on about 4 inches of gravel, followed by a 4-millimeter plastic sheet as a vapor barrier, and then the shed floor is built on top of it. (In fact, some she shed owners use the concrete for flooring, which is a further labor reduction.) Slabs are relatively easy to build and usually less expensive. But because they are resting on the ground, slabs can be affected by ground movement. Also they don't allow for natural air circulation beneath the floor, as do raised foundations.

Choosing the Right Kit

The number of shed kits offered by many companies is truly exciting to see. Your choices run the gamut from very basic prepackaged kits to highly customized sheds that allow you to specify special design features and materials. The level of detail and fancy features will affect the cost, of course.

Start with the major home improvement stores when looking for shed kits, but search also for the regional shed designers who "get" the she shed movement and are offering really attractive designs; many will also do the installation and building, if you want.

We went with a kit shed called the Everton. The shed comes with most of the pieces needed for completion, with the noted exclusion of finished flooring, paint, roofing materials, and foundation materials. There were about 85 different components, some in multiples, so keep in mind that you must keep track of hundreds of pieces. In the demonstration that follows, the kit includes lumber, (studs, beams, floor panels, roof joists, rafters, trim), panels (floor, roof, shelves), doors, and hardware (nails, door opener, door hinges, screws).

Budget

As noted in previous chapters, budgets for she sheds vary widely. It's possible to refurbish an old shed with donated materials, volunteer labor, and your own furnishings for under $100. Or you can hire a designer/builder to build a custom shed with plumbing, electrical service, and built-in cabinetry for upwards of $30,000. Only you can determine what you can afford—but part of the fun is seeing how close you can get to your dream she shed with the money you are willing to spend.

There are a few fixed costs and many, many variables to consider when building a she shed:

Stock kit vs. custom kit. Kit sheds like the one we used have many advantages, especially for novice builders. You get almost everything you need in one package and the wood is precut. The better ones aren't cheap, though: plan on spending at least $1,000 for a very small kit shed, and then probably another $500 to $1,000 on materials that aren't included.

Another option is to use a kit shed from a full-service shed designer and installer. This will cost you more because you are paying for materials, delivery, and labor for assembly and installation. Some of these sheds are pretty incredible, with handy features for a home office, art studio, or even a sleeping area. The companies are knowledgeable about sheds and can advise you as to site selection, weatherproofing, design, and finish details.

Custom sheds are basically built using your own design or that of a skilled builder or architect. If you can afford to spend more on your she shed, a custom design is great if you are trying to match your home or create a certain focal point on your property.

Unpack your kit carefully, and inventory and store the materials so they are easy to find when you need them during construction.

Restoring versus Building

Although this chapter is on building a new shed from a kit, we'll also pause for a moment to let you consider rejuvenating an old shed rather than building a new one. In most cases, if you have a shed already, you are going to spend less fixing it up than building one from scratch. If possible, keep the shed in the same place (assuming it has a nice solid foundation) and use the existing framework. You'll probably want to add windows, put in a new door, and make a lot of interior improvements.

Beware of rotting wood and old paint. Wood rot may start small but it will keep growing and the only way to stop it is by removing the affected piece altogether. Additionally, if your shed is 40 years old or more, it may have lead in the paint. Lead is very toxic if it is ingested or inhaled, especially for young children.

Materials. If free or donated materials are not an option, then you must factor in a materials budget. Building materials will include foundation materials, concrete, framing lumber, trim, hardware, paint, roof paper and shingles, windows, flooring, and whatever other materials are not included in the kit. See the Author's Case Study for an in-depth discussion of the kinds of material choices you may want to consider.

Labor and time constraints. This is probably one of the most important factors in budgeting money for a shed. The more time you or helpful friends and relatives have, the lower your costs are going to be. Here's why:

• Finding free or salvaged materials takes time and patience.

• You are able to work around the schedules of family and friends with day jobs who aren't always able to drop everything to help out.

• You can avoid paying extra for mistakes made along the way. For example, if the free window you found doesn't work, you just wait until you find another free one, instead of breaking down and purchasing a new one.

• You can stretch projects over a longer period of time and do them yourself, instead of hiring someone else.

There is a reason that humans band together to build structures: the work is difficult to do alone. Think of the traditional barn raising, when neighbors would gather at one farm to build an entire barn in a day. A shed raising will require at least a few friends and family members to help.

How much collective experience does your crew have? Although a shed is much less complicated than say, a house, it still requires basic building skills that some of us simply don't possess. In addition, you're also going to be moving and hauling heavy items, climbing on ladders, and holding heavy wood panels in place.

You should have a solid idea of the kind of shed you want and any extras you'll want to add (windows, special flooring, electrical, built-in furniture, front deck, etc.) and get it down on paper as a first step—a detailed sketch is always a good thing to have. Then talk to people in the building business to find out the kind of help and talent you will need.

It's fun to get the whole family involved and there are plenty of tasks that children can be assigned to do. Digging, painting, nailing panels, and framing are all tasks that can be handled by children eight years or older. They will always remember the summer that they built Mom's she shed.

Because our example shed was built on someone else's property, we didn't have the luxury of working on it a little bit here, a little bit there. We also didn't have a circle of personal friends that we could call on to help get the job done. If you don't have any building experience and don't know anyone else who does, you will probably have to seek the help of a professional builder or at the very least, a very capable handyman.

A Typical Shed Kit Assembly

The demonstration example that follows shows typical installation steps for one particular kit shed, but the principles are the same for most kit sheds you might purchase. But remember that with any shed, you're likely to want to make adaptations or variations to the standard kit. Later, in the Author's Case Study, you'll see the decision processes and installation adaptations we used for the windows, flooring, painting, and decorating of this she shed.

Each kit shed comes with instructions that you can download online as a PDF. Most kit manufacturers also offer telephone assistance if you need it—and don't be surprised if you do. Even the best kits may have problems with missing or incorrect parts, so don't be afraid to reach out for help. Your kit will come with hundreds of parts, so make sure you manage this inventory carefully, labeling and storing the parts so they are available when you need them.

Our demonstration shed required the following tools and materials:

Tools
- Air gun
- Caulk gun
- Clamps
- Hammer
- Handsaw
- Harness (for roof work)
- Jigsaw
- Ladder
- Level
- Painting tools (roller, brushes, pan, can opener, stir sticks)
- Paint sprayer
- Plumb bob with chalk line
- Power drill with bits
- Safety equipment (protective eyeglasses, gloves, hard hats, knee protectors)
- Sander
- Sawhorses
- Screwdriver, Philips
- Screwdriver, standard
- Staple gun
- Table saw
- T-square
- Utility knife

Materials
- Caulk
- Moisture-barrier plastic
- Nails
- Paint
- Primer
- Rain gutters and downspout
- Roofing shingles
- Roof paper
- Sandpaper
- Screws
- Wood glue

Building a Kit Shed:
The 13 Major Steps

1 Prepare the site. Lay a base of gravel about 4 inches thick and extending a little beyond the edges of the structure. Build the foundation—skid, slab, or raised. Shown here is a raised foundation with beams resting on the piers. The raised design accommodates the slope and allows for steps coming down from the entry.

2 Build the floor frame. Start with the outer rim joists, attaching them to the 4×4 beams, then install the interim joists so they span the rim joists at the designated spacing.

3 Assemble all your plywood floor panels (there are probably four of them). Lay them in place over the floor framing, flush with the edge of the frame and fasten with screws.

4 Construct each of the four wall panels, including window and door openings, flat on the ground, and lay them out on the building site near their intended locations. The window and door openings indicate where each wall should go.

5 Starting at the rear, position the back and left side wall upright onto the floor, keeping the wall exterior flush with the floor's edges. Attach the walls to one another at the corner with nails. Raise and join the remaining walls beginning with the right wall and moving to the front. Measure to make sure the wall frames are square, then attach them to the floor with nails. (To check for square, measure diagonals: equal measurements mean the framing is square. Install the walls' top plates as directed in the kit instructions.

6 Construct your roof rafters, positioning them first on the floor so that the angled tops fit together with full contact. Use glue and attach gussets to the peaks. Secure the gussets with 2-inch nails. Lift the rafters into position, one at a time. Align the rafters on the top plate, directly above the studs, and secure with 3-inch screws.

7 Attach the sheathing pieces to the framing with the included nails. Install the corner trim moldings and add whatever soffit and fascia trim is included with the kit. While most kits come with these moldings, some owners substitute more decorative trim for a custom look.

8 Attach the roof sheathing, starting with back panel, making sure it is square to the rafters. Install the rest of your roof panels, then cover the sheathing with roofing paper.

9 Paint your shed, inside and out. A pressure sprayer, like the one shown here, makes this work easier. Or, if your project is a family affair, painting is a job that younger members of the family may enjoy.

10 Hang the door as directed. Doors are another feature where you may want to customize the look with special trim or by cutting window openings, if your kit does not include them.

11 Install the windows, attaching them with nails driven through the nailing flanges and into the sheathing. Caulk liberally around the window openings to ensure the windows are airtight and your shed is usable in all weather.

12 Begin the finishing work by laying your desired flooring inside the shed and installing the desired roofing on the outside. These materials are usually not included with the shed kit, so here is your chance to give your shed a custom look. Now is also the time to add steps (if needed) and, if building on a raised foundation, to cover the space below the shed with lattice panels.

13 Now comes the real fun as you install accessories, including curtains and shelves, and create a unique design statement by decorating your shed with all the things that speak to your heart. Don't forget the landscaping!

Author's Case Study

Our demonstration shed was to be built on the property of my sister-in-law, Karin Nystrom, who lives almost 400 miles away from me and my husband, Tim. We were careful to plot out the time (accurately, we thought) it would take to assemble, build, paint, and furnish Karin's shed. We didn't have a lot of flexibility, because the great distance meant we couldn't spend an hour here or two hours there in between times catching up.

Our original schedule looked like this:

Weekend 1: Bring up some of the required tools and materials, set the piers, and lay out the foundation (treated 4×4 lumber). We hoped to also start the flooring joists and lay down the floor panels.

Weekend 2: A four-day weekend was planned to start immediately laying out a hardwood floor, constructing the walls, getting the roof panels in place, and ideally getting the roof tar paper stapled down. The third day would be laying down roofing shingles, framing and installing two windows, painting the shed inside and out, trimming, finishing the landscaping, and building the front steps. The final day would be the second polyurethane coat on the floor, then moving in the rugs, furnishings, artwork, and shelving.

The best-laid plans rarely go as hoped, though. The moral here is not to discourage you from building your own shed but to be flexible and understand that unforeseen circumstances are the norm, not the exception. In the real world, the schedule for Karin's shed went like this:

Weekend 1: A rainy week prior to the weekend caused some anxiety. Karin reported that the ground was very soggy and muddy. We drove up anyway and found that the soft ground actually was helpful for the digging we needed to do. The kit had been delayed in shipment; we wanted it there in order to check the pieces and measure it against the laid foundation, but we decided to go ahead without it.

Because the pier holes ended up being reset, the foundation took longer than expected. We completed the piers and beams before heading home.

Weekend 2: The kit was delivered about two days before our arrival; that was close! We began to move all of the pieces into Karin's backyard. The shed has about 85 different components, and it took about an hour to organize. By the end of the first day we had the floor, walls, and roof beams complete.

The second day we lost Charlie, one of our neighbor helpers, to care for his sick wife. Things went a little more slowly as a result. We hoped to get all of the siding and trim in place so that Karin's friend Gregory could start painting. A slight mishap on the roof involving nails that were a bit too long and sticking through the ceiling took us off track once again.

We spent a few weeks researching shed kits and ended up deciding on an Everton wood shed that measures 8×12 feet. The kit was delivered on a pallet, and we then needed to unpack and organize the pieces. A garage is ideal for this, but we had to make do with the back porch.

We finished the siding and trim the morning of the third day, except for the loft shelf (we chose to use sturdier wood than what was provided in the kit, so we hand-painted it later on). While Gregory and Karin painted, we started papering and shingling the roof. This part of the shed building took a long time, as it was just my husband, my thirteen-year-old son, and me.

We had to leave the shed unfinished and schedule one final weekend to get it done.

Weekend 3: While Charlie finished the windows, we laid out the vinyl flooring. This turned out to be a pleasant surprise, as it was very easy to do, took only a couple of hours, and looked great. (See "Author's Workshop: Flooring Choices" to see why we gave up on hardwood.) Then we spent the rest of the day on landscaping. Charlie built the front steps while Tim worked on cutting lattice (already spray-painted by Gregory) to fit around the exposed piers of the foundation. We designed a simple pathway and filled it with pea gravel.

The second day was move-in day. Tim built a handsome worktop out of a pine slab and metal brackets, as well as a few display shelves from scrap wood. Karin and I moved in all of the furnishings, artwork, and decorative elements we had stored in her dining room for the past month.

We had just enough time to photograph the end result in the late-afternoon sun before packing up our tools and heading home one final time.

TIP

Do a trial run first, using stakes and 2×4s to make sure the position of the shed on the building site will work—avoid our mistake. We forged ahead and dug all the holes for the piers (the posts at each corner of the shed that support it) and installed the piers before Karin realized the angle of the shed was not quite right, which required us to dig and install new piers.

The wall frames are built flat on the ground then brought to the shed for installation.

Tim oversees Dana as he drives screws into the wall base.

Lessons Learned

Here are some important things you can learn from our own experience (and yes, a few mistakes):

• Stay grounded in reality. The images you see of finished sheds are often highly stylized and edited. They show a conceptual idea of the shed in ideal conditions, not the shed that will be in your kit. That's fine as long as you don't have unrealistic expectations and know that you have to put a lot of your own materials into the project to make it look the way you want.

• Consider size. To use your shed as an actual studio or room, it will need to be at least 6×8 feet. Even that is on the small side. Look for shed designs with good ceiling height and front porches for livability.

• Shed kits aren't perfect. We were very happy with the style and features of our shed, but there were pieces that were warped and unusable. Be prepared to buy replacement pieces as you go.

• It takes a village. At least for us, it did. Our team of family and friends included my husband, who is a very accomplished hobbyist builder, me and my two children (few skills), and Karin. We encountered our share of glitches, delays, and frustrations. Luckily, two of Karin's friends pitched in. It took us six full days to build the shed.

• Just because it's a DIY project doesn't mean a she shed can be built effortlessly in a day. Any structure that is going to be "lived in" by a human will take time, skill, and patience. There are going to be steps in the instruction booklet that will seem incomprehensible. There will be do-overs. There will be paint, sawdust, and dirt.

• Keep gas in the car. You're going to be taking lots of trips to the local home improvement store during the build.

• Planning to paint your shed? A paint sprayer will be your best friend. We loved having both the exterior and interior completely painted in maybe two hours. Make sure you have someone on your crew who knows how to use and care for the sprayer.

Customizing Your Windows

Kit sheds are still designed with storage in mind rather than for a human being who is actually using it for an extra room—that means windows will either not be part of the plan at all or that the provided windows may be of lesser quality than you would find in an actual home.

You are without a doubt going to want windows added to your shed. Windows and glass doors are probably the single most transformational design element for a she shed—they make the space feel larger and provide natural light that is important especially if you choose not to add electricity.

For Karin's shed, we found two large windows of extraordinarily high quality. These matching windows came from a construction project where the client ended up choosing a different style and could not return them. They were on for sale on Craigslist and became ours for $150. The windows came complete with a nailing flange (or nail fin), ideal for new construction.

When the right and left walls were framed out and mounted to the floor, we determined the space where the windows would go. The tops of the windows needed to be close to the base of the roof; otherwise, Karin would have to stoop to see out of them. We set them as high as we could but then found we had introduced a problem: the windows, which are casement and swing outward on hinges, couldn't clear the rafter ends overhanging on the outside of the shed.

We had to adjust the rough opening by moving it down a few inches so that the window could swing out and let in the fresh air. Bonus: the windows had screens too!

The windows we found came ready to install with a frame and a nailing flange. They were on the large side for a shed this size, so we had to be careful about positioning them just right and had to alter the wall framing to accommodate them.

Seen from the interior, the windows open out using a handle and look great with the rest of the shed. We faced the top edge with a stained pine board and used that as a base for the curtain rod.

Flooring Choices

Choosing your flooring is fun because you have so many great options. To narrow it down, consider your overall style, the use (or abuse) your floor likely will endure, the level of difficulty to install, and, of course, your budget. The good news regarding budget is that because most shed floors are not very large, you don't have to buy a lot of product.

Here are some of the common types of flooring to consider:

Wood. True wood floors feel good on the feet and are deeply attractive to most people. They are also the most expensive, unless you use salvage or get them donated. Hardwood needs to be installed over a plywood subfloor; it cannot be installed directly over concrete. If you're planning to use your shed for gardening, you probably want to choose flooring that doesn't mind water, such as concrete or even fine gravel.

Carpet. Wall-to-wall carpet that you see in a house is a rarity in she sheds; there is just too much risk of dampness and rot. However, natural fiber carpeting such as sisal or seagrass are options to consider. Another idea is to paint your plywood subfloor with floor paint, then use colorful throw rugs. Rugs are nice because they can be pulled up, washed, and aired out.

Vinyl. Vinyl has come a long way in the last ten years, offering designs and textures that closely resemble natural materials such as wood, brick, and stone. Vinyl can be installed over plywood or concrete, as long as the surface is smooth and dry. You can use self-adhesive vinyl squares or large sheets, which are cut to fit and set with adhesive. A newer option is floating vinyl planks, which you simply "click" into place using interlocking tongues and grooves.

Laminate. Laminate flooring is plank or tile product in which a decorative plastic surface finish is bonded to a particleboard or manufactured wood backing. Just like vinyl, laminates are very easy to install and can convincingly mimic the look of wood, tile, stone, and other materials. They are a cost effective and very popular choice for flooring. Some products are glued down, but most use a "floating" installation method in which interlocking tongues and grooves are clicked into place.

Brick. Bricks are actually used as a material for both foundations and floors, and they are a warm, extremely attractive material to consider for your shed. Lay your brick with the broad side up or on edge, using sand as the base and between the bricks to keep them in place. While they are

The vinyl plank flooring we used was very easy to cut and install. All of the instructions were listed on the box.

sturdy, bricks are still porous, so use a sealer on them.

Cement. If you're building your shed on a concrete slab, then the slab can do double duty as your floor too! Consider staining it for an ultra-modern, loft-in-the-city effect; you can also finish it with an epoxy coating—a resin product used for garage and shop floors that is extremely durable and also comes in many colors and textures.

Tile. Nothing beats tile for its toughness against water and moisture—that's why it's in all of our bathrooms. Tile is a beautiful, classic floor surface that is a bit labor intensive to install. It is also a bit pricier. Again, consider that you have a small area to cover and if the installation is done well, your tile will last a very long time.

When we first began planning Karin's shed, the flooring was going to be hardwood. My husband and I had a stack of beautiful Rose River Gum flooring that we've had for years after remodeling a previous home. We had almost enough for the 96 square feet, and just purchased a few lengths of remnant wood for about $20 that we would use on the outer edges. All of it would be stained and varnished to look the same.

As time went on, however, two things reshaped our plan. First, our window of time shrank. Prepping wood for a floor installation must be done piece by piece, very carefully. You also should season the wood in the room for at least a week so that the moisture within the wood balances with the air moisture. We worried about how we could fit it into our schedule and we were still down one helper.

Secondly, Karin began to worry about how the hardwood floor would fare in her rainy climate.

The end result looks (almost) like hardwood floors. We finished off the edges with scrap wood baseboards.

We took time to treat the plywood subfloor with a liquid concrete paint and a plastic moisture barrier. We even rented a hardwood floor nailer but had to finish up walls, roof, and painting first and never got around to using it. We went home that second weekend with the floor still not finished.

The experience taught us an important lesson: know when to let go. We gave up on the idea of hardwoods and discussed alternative flooring that would have the same look but was easier to install. The answer was a floating vinyl plank flooring system. One of Karin's neighbors uses it in all of the apartment buildings he owns and was impressed by its durability and decent resemblance to true wood. After buying a few packs on his contractor's discount, we set to work.

The floor was astonishingly easy to install, and very quick. This was a smart decision and allowed us to catch up to where we needed to be on that final weekend. To finish off the edges, we made a quick baseboard/shoe molding out of scrap wood.

Painting Tips

Painting is one of the most satisfying parts of customizing a she shed. It's also a little bit scary. Do you go safe or crazy? Pastel or bright? Playful or edgy? It may be just a shed but it's also going to be an important part of your life . . . and your yard.

Karin spent many hours looking at paint swatches and deciding whether or not she wanted the shed color to match the color of her home. In the end, Pinterest pointed her in the right direction. She spotted a chocolate brown shed with a contrasting door in a deep purple and fell in love with the look. Her friend and paint consultant, Gregory LeBaron of Transformational Color, helped out by pointing out subtle differences in color and how colors will change at different times of the day.

One of the biggest timesavers we used was the paint sprayer. Gregory waited until all of the wall panels, trim pieces, and caulking were complete before starting. Then, he and Karin worked together starting with the interior. Primer went on first, followed by a cream color. Gregory sprayed using quick, even strokes; Karin followed behind with a paint roller to take care of any uneven applications.

The sprayer was cleaned out, and then we painted the exterior. Karin handled the sprayer this time and got the hang of it quickly. Since the paint is being pushed out with so much force, it provides great coverage and we only needed one coat of brown to finish the job.

A few practical matters regarding the paint job:

1. You should always use a primer before painting bare wood and particleboard. Primer will even out the surface and make the wood less porous. In addition, the paint will bond well to the primer and last longer.

2. If you are painting the floor, use a paint formulated for flooring. These paints are more durable to resist chipping and scuff marks from foot traffic.

3. Renovating an old shed? Remember that old paint applied before 1970 could contain lead. Do not let children sand or remove paint and it is best to have a professional come in to remove it safely.

The paint sprayer really helped us save time, especially since we had a smaller crew than we expected, and the resulting paint job was beautiful.

Primer was applied first to the bare wood inside the shed. Gregory handled the paint sprayer and Karin used a roller where necessary to even out the paint.

The Fun Stuff

After laying the vinyl plank flooring, it was time for Karin and I to fill the shed with her furnishings. While we mapped out a design, Tim worked on the worktop and the display shelves.

The first thing to go in the shed was a large, soft, green area rug that was a new purchase. As to furniture, Karin had two large pieces that she really liked: a wooden day bed and a large futon chair that was the first piece of furniture she ever bought as a college student. We discovered that both of them made the shed too crowded. We opted for the futon and fit it diagonally into the back left corner. Slipcovered in cream matelasse and punctuated with accent pillows, the futon could do double duty as a small guest bed.

A tall, round table went on the other side, covered with a piece of bright cloth. A forgotten IKEA side table became a companion piece for the futon. Window treatments were two hand-woven textiles that were given to Karin while she taught in Indonesia. They were simply swagged over two small curtain rods.

Everything chosen for the shed was a treasured piece or something that she had been hanging onto in hopes of finding just the right place for. The futon had been at her mother's home for thirty years. Many of the art pieces and accessories reflect Karin's love of Indonesia and her many travels.

Near the doorway, the worktop was installed along with two matching shelves above it. We used metal brackets from a home improvement store. The chair is an extra dining room chair that Karin didn't need in the house. The finishing touch is a small chandelier set high in the rafters, which was in one of my daughter's rooms when she was little.

Finished at last! As we cleaned up our tools and the sawdust, Karin's shed glowed in the late afternoon sunlight. It was a lot of work and filled with unexpected challenges, but as we gazed at the she shed that we built ourselves, we felt the deep satisfaction of a job well done.

(Above) We were delighted with how this basic kit shed turned out. Customizing with windows, paint, and decorative details make such a big difference in the final outcome.

(Right, top) A large futon chair is the primary piece of furniture in Karin's shed. There is enough room for it to extend out as a bed. The handy loft shelf provides space for storage.

(Right, bottom) No-sew swags are pieces of fabric draped over small curtain rods.

Karin will use her worktop for journaling and she also brought out some of her art and travel reference books.

Simple display shelves were made with scrap wood stained the same as the work table. Karin places antique bottles that belonged to her late husband.

By late afternoon of our final shed-building weekend, the final result exceeded our expectations. Spacious and sturdy, Karin's she shed will serve her well as a retreat, mini guest house, and adjunct home office.

8 | *Gallery*

There's something special about every she shed, and this chapter provides another look at why they appeal so to our spirits and imaginations. She shed ownership fosters an amazing spirit of community. Hundreds of Facebook groups, Pinterest boards, blogging communities, forums, and Houzz members exist and flourish for the sheer enjoyment of comparing notes on designing, building, improving, sharing, and enjoying their sheds.

Consider this a gallery of ideas and impressions. Elements of these sheds may provide you with just the right inspiration as you do your research. The more you look at them, the more ideas come to mind about all of the essential elements of good she shed living: construction, design, style, site selection, color, function, and, yes, livability. Explore these well designed and versatile structures, from classic to modern, and use the inspiration to help you build a she shed of your own.

Audrey's Teahouse

Audrey's teahouse reflects the widespread appeal of this ancient Asian practice of using a small private building for the ceremonial pouring of tea. Here the structure is modernized, intended as a substantial focal point for an extensive yard with a large pond and waterfall. It was designed by architect Jerry Eschman, who used only a very old photo of a Bali teahouse for inspiration. Eschman designed a mortise-and-tenon structure joined with wood pegs, a traditional and very strong method of frame construction.

One of the shed's important distinguishing characteristics is its roof. Both the ridge of the roof and the rafters curve up slightly at the ends, something that Eschman noticed on the structure in the photo. This more than anything else captured the spirit of the place. Beyond that he added thoroughly modern features for comfort and for harmonious balance with the house. French doors and large multi-paned windows reach almost floor to ceiling to make the teahouse feel wide open. The teahouse sits on a raised foundation of concrete topped with slate and faced with dry stacked stone.

Audrey's teahouse was designed for pure relaxation and enjoyment. It is intentionally situated on a rise to command sweeping views of the water and gardens. From a long-ago hut in Bali, a modern-day teahouse emerges.

Photography: Jerry Eschman

(Right) Unique features of the teahouse include gently curving roof ridges and rafters, as well as decorative carving on the rafter tails and bargeboard.

(Opposite) Audrey's teahouse is a modern interpretation of an old Bali thatched structure. Using thoroughly modern materials and mortise-and-tenon construction, this wonderful little house anchors the entire yard. Architect Jerry Eschman used standard window sizes to cut down on costs.

Studio Sheds

In response to the growing notion that sheds are not just for storage anymore, Studio Sheds came to the fore. These pre-fabricated, customizable sheds have the look of an uber-cool addition you might build on a contemporary house, giving the remarkable appearance of a professionally designed space.

At the core of the Studio Shed concept is a construction method utilizing products and techniques that are sturdy, economical, and less wasteful. Engineered wood is the base material selected for its strength as well as its sustainability. Because engineered wood products are created using more of the timber parts, such as tree fibers that are typically left to waste, they are extremely efficient. They also provide more consistent structural integrity due to the reconstitution process (i.e. no knots or cracks). All of the lumber used is FSC certified, which means that it passes criteria on how and where the lumber was harvested in order to better protect forests and ecosystems.

In addition to the wood, these sheds are designed with a distinct window trim made of metal. The metal used within the window construction and as trim is fabricated to each shed's specification and all scrap metal is reused. Insulation is made with recycled denim, and the flooring is cork.

From one core structural plan comes an impressive array of options that allow each she shed owner to personalize the pre-fab. The company's online 3D Configurator allows you to design your shed by selecting size, layout, color, siding, accessories, and foundation type. As always, select with care, and get all your questions answered before moving forward.

Photography: Studio Sheds

Streamlined in Seattle

A Seattle-based artist was priced out of her downtown art studio and began looking around for another solution. Since she was a large-format painter, her work gets messy, and she requires plenty of space to move around. There was a tiny studio on the property, and it germinated the idea of a larger shed—a less expensive way to provide all the room and light she needed. Modern Shed is the company that she selected to create the design. The attractive palette of deep gray and tomato red on walls and trim is a close match to the house, and the shed design was modified to fit the very steep slope in the yard. Inside, a cubby system holds many rolled-up works in progress; otherwise, floor space reigns.

Clever entryways and decking convert a "plopped-down" shed into one that is truly integrated into its surroundings. You can opt for simple extras like a stairstep, or shift to a more indoor/outdoor configuration by building a full porch or deck, partitions, pergolas, or fencing. What turns an ordinary shed into a place for living and creativity are elements that connect the structure to its environment. Companies like Modern Shed will usually provide services for add-ons and provide expert consultation.

Photography: Dominic Bonuccelli

(Right) The metal wall panels install quickly and are prefabricated at the company's facility. The lightning-speed construction of this shed leaves time for creating a spectacular entrance. Stylish Arts-and-Crafts fencing is characterized by large 4×4-inch square posts, with the frame painted the same gray as the shed, and, for contrast, stained wood rails and decking.

(Opposite) Perched on a steep slope, this she shed was the answer to an artist's quest for light-filled space in which to work on large-format pieces. Much of the pier foundation was clad in the same dark-gray metal paneling as the walls, for a graceful, continuous elevation.

Modern Meets Historic

There are many alternative terms for a she shed and here's another one to add: Alternative Dwelling Unit, or ADU. This is a planner's term for a fully livable (and professionally designed) second unit that is part of a larger owned property. Sheila Meehan's 10×12-foot shed was the answer to a dilemma she faced as the owner of an historic home with no room for her work as a licensing agent for artists. "There were two deciding factors that made us choose a shed," Meehan says. "The cost was affordable without having to refinance our home, and the speed to a finished product was impressive."

The shed (from Modern Shed) is very modern in its minimalist structure and low sloping roofline. Yet its clever color palette of sage green and slate gray suited Meehan's 1925 home, so that it felt like a natural extension. An architect helped determine the best site for the shed, as well as where the doors and windows should be. Within a few days, Meehan's homey new office was ready for move-in.

Photography: Dominic Bonuccelli

Inside, the features are simple but attractive. The walls are birch, which come standard with the shed. Meehan selected locally grown bamboo for her flooring and also selected her own lighting, which the shed company installed for her. She decided to use her own furnishings instead of making built-ins, so that she could move things around as she wished.

Made entirely with modern and eco-friendly materials, Meehan's shed nevertheless reflects the spirit of her ninety-year-old home. It fits snugly within her small backyard and allows her the quiet and privacy she needs to run her business.

The Literary Cabin

Nestled in the woods of the North Shore of Lake Superior, Ann Possis's she shed evokes the classic fairy tale cottage. Possis's former husband built it for her so that she could have a place of her own—he just acquired his own office above their new garage. They converted an old shed that had rotted almost to the ground. Original components include the great double doors, which close over the glass doors when desired.

The interior is illuminated with ten windows, including two additional stained glass panels and glass sidelights flanking the front door. The original ceiling boards were painted sky blue, and the shelves, desk, and trim all have a pale white stain. After unsuccessfully trying to stain the floorboards (and using many choice words in the process), Possis settled for dark green porch paint.

The shed is not insulated, so it is purely a summer place. However, it is wired for electricity and for phone service so that Possis can use it as a home office.

Photography: Ann Possis

Possis and her carpenter designed the interior of the shed, including the shelving, brackets, and an L-shaped desk for making paper art cards. The shed is a great place for reading, too; the shelves are filled with books that go back to Possis's childhood.

Ann Possis's rustic she shed was fashioned from an old tool shed. A local carpenter jacked it up and built a new foundation on piers; Possis reused as much of the old materials as she could. The result is a shed that feels at one with its surroundings.

Recycled Green- houses

A unique business in central California designs and builds "functional art" in the form of spacious and light-filled she sheds. A Place to Grow/Recycled Greenhouses structures are characterized by a heavy use of reclaimed wood, including one hundred-year-old barn wood, torn-down wood fences and even recycled wine flavor sticks (pieces of wood used to flavor wine as it ages in the barrel).

Very little new lumber is used in the construction of these sheds; as a result, the wood species and color will often vary from shed to shed, or even wall to wall. Other materials are also used in the construction process, such as corrugated metal and polycarbonate panels. The result is an eclectic construction that is nevertheless extremely sturdy and utterly unique.

Once the design is determined, materials are sourced directly from Recycled Greenhouses' warehouse. Over the years, they have accumulated a huge inventory of materials salvaged from demolition, remodels, and lumber mills. Clients can come in and select from hundreds of salvaged doors and windows, but they can also use anything of their own and have it integrated into the design. Then the entire shed is designed, cut, and brought to the site for installation.

Photography: Kim Snyder/kimberlyjoysnyder.com

(Left, top) The sewing shed windows are reclaimed, with wood frames and real divided lites.

(Left, bottom) The interior is a hospitable space with a table for tea and a soft area rug underfoot. The walls are outfitted with plenty of shelves and display cabinets to hold the owner's myriad collections of glassware and vintage figurines.

(Opposite, top) Dog-ear fence boards nailed upside down create a whimsical scalloped pattern across the front gable of this she shed. Note the overhang of the roof extends out far enough to create a shelter over the front porch.

(Opposite, bottom) Two beautifully crafted full-size doors were salvaged and put together to create a wide entrance to this shed, which is used as a sewing room. Several large tables provide plenty of work surface for projects—and no one complains if the mess is left out to be worked on another day.

The Little Red Shed

This cheery red shed is the perfect example of how the surrounding landscape should be an extremely important consideration when determining a location. While the shed here provides a substantial focal point for the outer edge of the property and is attractive in and of itself, you can see how much the environs matter.

A large yard like this one is often divided into various sections, with interesting plantings and pathways that encourage the eye to wander in several directions. Here the meandering flagstone pathways lead through and around a raised "island" of succulents and palms, with the main pathway heading towards the shed. Flaming pink bougainvillea is planted near the shed and it will eventually frame the entrance.

Photography: Gabriel Frank/Gardens by Gabriel

At the far end of this beautifully landscaped yard is a simple classic shed, painted oxblood red with white trim. It makes for a quiet and secluded retreat and feels quite at home within the garden design. The owner furnished it with a small pine armoire, an antique round table, a day bed with lots of pillows, and a small vintage chandelier.

French Farmhouse Style

What exactly connotes a French farmhouse? It is a style that is both rustic and sophisticated, earthy, and colorful. Nearly half of France's land is still used for agriculture, and the people take pride in their locally farmed products. So it's no surprise that this Old World style is appealing to people in the rest of the world, as well.

This gardening shed is an interpretation of what a humble shed might look like in context with the French farmhouse, which is often constructed of stone and plaster. Note the wide barn wall siding, set vertically on a short foundation of gray stone, and the exposed rafter beams inside. A large French door is framed simply in unpainted wood trim, and complemented by large multi-lite windows. Although designed to appear rustic, the shed's meticulous finish work and pristine appearance give away the fact that it was intentionally designed and built for a contemporary taste.

Photography: M-Buck Studio LLC

This French farmhouse-inspired gardening shed offers a pleasant and sheltered place for both the serious gardener and the novice. The exposed rafters and joists as well as Provence terra cotta tile flooring contribute to its pastoral appeal. Pea gravel walkways are also a quintessential French touch.

Old-Fashioned Cottage

Once upon a time, when we were small, we dreamed of a yellow cottage with white trim where we lived happily ever after. For the woman who never quite outgrew her love of playhouses, this steeply gabled clapboard shed is irresistible, especially since it looks like a miniature version of a real house. Although measuring just 12×12 feet, the shed seems spacious because of the high, sloped ceiling. It is actually used for a number of crafting and art projects by the owner and has a large loft space for storage (after her daughter outgrew it as a reading nook). The wide French doors allow her to bring in furniture pieces that need restoration.

A small gable roof over the front entryway mirrors the shape of the shed's roof, creating a classic cottage look. To further embellish this theme, tiny porch posts and gingerbread millwork on the gable are important details if you are going for a look that is less shed and more house.

The Victorian style isn't for everyone. Some consider it too fussy and not harmonious with the natural surroundings. Nevertheless, this cottage shows restraint in its ornamentation and could suit any kind of property. It is truly the feminine she shed of the imagination.

Photography: Pamela/flowerpatchgardens.com

(Right) Built in the classic cottage style, this she shed is a practical studio with good light and space. The roof is corrugated metal, and the walls were super insulated to keep the shed warm during the winter months. In the summertime, the owner's abundant flowerbeds create a pretty framework around the creamy yellow shed.

(Opposite) Inside the cottage is the look of a little house that has been lived in for many years—beadboard walls and double-hung windows both contribute to the vintage cottage style. Vinyl flooring has the look of Victorian black-and-white tile. Freestanding furniture includes a handsome painted armoire in mint green and white.

Belle of the Garden

Sheds are often designed and built to be decorative on the outside while covering up a practical storage area on the inside. Still, in some cases it ends up being considered more than just a tool shed by the woman owner of the house. This is what happened with this grand she shed, dubbed Williamsburg Gardenbelle, that sits in an award-winning garden near Greenwich, Connecticut.

The owner wanted an historic-looking shed to anchor a walled vegetable garden. This shed design, from Garden Sheds Inc., was inspired by the architecture of Colonial Williamsburg, with its somewhat austere and tidy aesthetic of tall, narrow brick or clapboard buildings, narrow divided-lite windows, and paint colors in neutral shades of white, gray, brown, or dark green. It was exactly what she wanted, with a few key custom touches that made it unique.

Whimsical details make this she shed a standout and not so austere. First, it is hexagonal in shape and features small eave brackets spaced at short intervals. Topping things off is a wonderful ogee roof (slight *S* curvature), with high-profile asphalt shingles and a ball-and-spike finial for good measure. The end result was so pretty that the owner puts candles around the shed for parties so that it glows.

Photography: Stacy Bass Photography

Twin trellises support the garden's climbing roses on the Williamsburg Gardenbelle she shed. This impressive architectural structure is actually centered within the brick wall and becomes part of the landscape's permanence.

Resources

Your she shed research will take you down many paths, which is part of the fun in planning this intensely personal space. Special gratitude goes to the community at Houzz (www.houzz.com), an online gathering place where architects, interior designers, and ordinary people share photos and stories of their home-remodeling projects. A meticulous user interface and elegant search and organizing functions make this site one of the most useful for discovering both professional and DIY she shed projects.

The resources listed here provide more information, when available, about the owners and the designers of the sheds in this book.

Chapter 2
"Corncrib Conversion" (page 20)
Styling: Charlotte Safavi
Interior Design: Jamie Merida
Architect: Jon Braithwaite
Landscape Design: Geoffrey C. Stone

Chapter 3
"From Greenhouse to Glitterfarm" (page 42)
A Place to Grow (recycled greenhouses),
    www.recycledgreenhouses.com
Glitterfarm, www.glitterfarm.com

"Cindy's Shed by the Sea" (page 50)
Landscape Designer: Olaf von Sperl,
    www.adoremygarden.com
Cindy Goode Milman, www.cindygoodemilman.com
Shelter (green roof plans), www.greenroofplans.com

"Clare's Sewing Sanctuary" (page 62)
Oxfordshire shed from Creative Living,
    www.creativelivingcabins.co.uk

"Tool Shed Transforms" (page 66)
The Gilded Gypsies, www.thegildedgypsies.blogspot.com

"Studio for Sketching" (page 72)
Gardensheds, www.gardensheds.com
Outbuildings, www.outbuildings.com
Barn lights, www.barnlightelectric.com

Chapter 4
"Allie's Hen Hut" (page 78)
Santa Barbara Home Designer,
    www.santabarbarahomedesigner.com

"Salvaged She Shed" (page 90)
Living Vintage, www.livingvintageco.com

Chapter 5
"Spanish-Style She Shed" (page 96)
Santa Barbara Home Designer,
    www.santabarbarahomedesigner.com

Chapter 6
"The Tacking Shed" (page 112)
Gardensheds, www.gardensheds.com
Outbuildings, www.outbuildings.com

"My Own Little Cabin" (page 120)
Santa Barbara Home Designer,
    www.santabarbarahomedesigner.com

Chapter 7
Paint consultation: Gregory LeBaron of Transformational
    Color, www.transformationalcolor.com

Chapter 8
Studio Sheds, www.studio-shed.com

Modern Sheds, www.modern-shed.com

A Place to Grow/Recycled Greenhouses,
    www.recycledgreenhouses.com

Gardens by Gabriel, www.gardensbygabriel.com

Flower Patch Gardens Cottage Plans,
    www.flowerpatchgardens.com

Gardensheds, www.gardensheds.com

Outbuildings, www.outbuildings.com

Index

About the Author

Erika Kotite is a magazine editor and book developer, contributing to numerous titles for major book publishers. The former editor of *Romantic Homes* and *Victorian Homes*, Erika became a partner in a book packaging company, working within the arts, textile, and crafting sectors. Some of her primary book projects include *Blogging for Bliss, Crowns & Tiaras, Natural Soapmaking, Natural Candlemaking, Photo Album Quilts, Felt Fashion,* and *The Daily Book of Photography.*

Erika and her husband have restored and remodeled several of their historic homes through the years, including a 1920s Los Angeles Tudor, a 1938 fishing shack in Marin County, and an eighteenth-century general store/post office in Lambertville, New Jersey. She served on the Hopewell Township Historic Preservation Commission from 2008 to 2011.

Erika is currently editor-in-chief of the Beauty Group at Bobit Business Media. She lives in Huntington Beach, California, with her husband and three children.